LOOK, MOM—I CAN FLY!

Memoirs of a World War II P-38 Fighter Pilot

Robert "Smoky" Vrilakas

To Dale + Jim

With many thanks for your interest in
a slice of WW II history

Robert "Smoky" Vrilakas

AMETHYST MOON
PUBLISHING

Look Mom—I Can Fly!

Cover photo courtesy of Lockheed Martin

An Amethyst Moon Book
Published by AMETHYST MOON PUBLISHING
P.O. Box 87885
Tucson, AZ 85754
www.ampubbooks.com

This book is available in these formats:
Paperback: ISBN 978-1-935354-47-5 / 1-935354-47-7
eBook (epub): ISBN 978-1-935354-89-5 / 1-935354-89-2
eBook (mobi): ISBN 978-1-935354-90-1 / 1-935354-90-6

First Edition 2011

Library of Congress Control Number: 2012900739

This memoir is the author's recollections, impressions, and memories of the actual events as they occurred.

Look, Mom—I Can Fly!

Memoirs of a World War II P-38 Fighter Pilot

Robert "Smoky" Vrilakas

Dedication

To those I flew with and to those who did not return.

Contents

Introduction

The day I was to fly a P-38 fighter for the first time arrived in mid-April 1943. It was springtime at Muroc Army Air Base in the Southern California Mohave Desert, the kind of day that Mohave Desert dwellers liked to talk about. It was cloudless, at a very comfortable temperature, and visibility so crystal clear that the distant mountains surrounding the desert appeared to be just a few miles away. The day was in sharp contrast to midsummer, when flying there often had to be done in the morning. The afternoon desert sun on a metal airplane made it too hot to touch, let alone seal oneself in the cockpit.

Having completed both basic army infantry and air corps training, I was at my life's best physical condition. There were, however, the accompanying internal doubts that brought goose bumps, such as: "Are you really ready for this," and "are you sure you were meant to do this?" This was a different kind of introduction to an airplane. The single-seated cockpit and only one set of flight controls did not permit hands-on learning from a flight instructor. All that must be learned had to be learned in the classroom, by oral instruction on the ground, and from the aircraft flight manual. Further, the condition of the P-38s we were to fly was not the best. They were older models with high flying time on them. Mechanical failures had become somewhat commonplace. The men who maintained them were in the learning process, the same as we pilots. There had been an abnormal number of engine failures in flight, which to the novice P-38 pilot presented a daunting challenge. Too often, a novice experiencing an engine failure on takeoff would end up in a crash landing off the runway; the emergency procedure had to be right in such a case or the consequences could be serious. Loss of an engine in flight also required precise procedures by the pilot to shut down the dead engine, maintain control of the aircraft, and bring it in for a safe landing. This was demonstrated quite vividly during our training when two P-38s

crashed almost simultaneously due to engine failures, one burning at
each end of the runway. Some crashes resulted in pilot fatalities; others
forced, or persuaded, the trainee to leave the program. (Realistic flight
simulators available now, but not then, would have virtually eliminated
this problem.)

You can't dwell on those kinds of negatives and fly, so I put all of that
out of mind and surveyed the P-38s, all in a row on the flight line. They
looked beautiful—parked with the nose of the plane slightly elevated
as if they couldn't wait to get in the air. My instructor accompanied
me to my assigned P-38 and crawled up on the wing as I buckled in.
Taxi instructions from the tower, sounding somewhat paternal to a
"newbie," cleared me to the takeoff position near the end of the runway.
My instructor then rode on my wing as I taxied out. He suggested that
I take it up to at least 6,000 feet, get the feel of the plane, and then
practice shutting down an engine to include "feathering" the propeller
on the dead engine. Feathering a dead engine propeller by turning the
blades horizontal to the air stream is essential to stop engine rotation and
reduces drag on the aircraft.

While taxiing, to maintain hydraulic pressure and keep the brakes
available, it was necessary to continually pump the rudder pedals with
one's feet. By the time the takeoff location was reached at the end of the
runway my legs felt like lead weights. One's legs built up to the strain
after a few flights, but a year later when I became an instructor in P-38s
I could tell it was happening to my first-flight students. The twin rudders
on their P-38 would flutter as they reached the end of the runway for
takeoff. The flutter was caused by their legs shaking with fatigue as they
pumped the rudder pedals. I'm sure my rudders were doing a dance. At
the end of the runway my instructor made sure all latches were secure,
gave me a reassuring thumbs-up, and slid off the wing to the ground.

I was now on my own.

It was reminiscent of my first solo flight almost a year prior in a
bi-wing fabric-covered PT-17, except that now my head was crammed

with a thousand more thoughts about systems operation, emergency procedures, flap, throttle, tachometer, airspeed, and control settings—plus endless advice on what to do and not to do. On top of that was the task of trying to guide and control the newest warplane in the military, something that could reach speeds I, and many other pilots, had never experienced.

Following preflight, engine run-up, and final checklist, I requested clearance from the tower to proceed on to the runway. A matter-of-fact and professional voice from the tower cleared me to taxi on to the runway and to take off.

In takeoff position, the final blow to my legs came as I pumped the brakes to hold the airplane and applied full power—the engines revved up to full power and stabilized. When it seemed the legs couldn't take another second of this kind of punishment, I released the brakes and the P-38 shot forward like a drag racer. It continued to accelerate rapidly to lift off speed, about 90 miles per hour, and responded like a well-trained race horse to my commands as it became airborne. I was so busy getting gear and flaps up, stabilizing power, checking engine instruments and my airspeed that I was at 4,000 feet and doing 260 miles per hour before realizing it. It had taken to the sky like a homesick angel. Confidence in my ability to fly the P-38 began to take charge. It flew beautifully as I put it through a series of air maneuvers to learn how it would respond. The pilot's seat in a P-38 is in the center of the wings, and that position gave the pilot a feeling of being part of the airplane, with the wings an extension of the arms. The anxiety factor was there, as it is for everyone flying a plane for the first time, but it was "love at first flight." At that time, I was only about a mile above the Southern California desert, but further from my childhood and my home than I ever could have imagined.

Chapter 1—George and May

My father, George Vrilakas, was born in Rethymnon, on the Greek island of Crete, on April 14, 1885, to a large family of eight children. His father was the equivalent of a town mayor and was, from what I could gather, a strong-willed authoritarian who ruled the town and his family under rigid standards. His son George, with a somewhat chiseled facial profile and prominent eyebrows, personified the Cretan character. He was slight of build, wiry, but very strong and energetic for his size. He had no fear of the unknown and was never hesitant about taking any job offer or pursuing any line of work. Also characteristic of his Cretan heritage, he was fiercely independent.

At age 22, after an altercation with his father, George and a friend found passage on a ship and sailed to what he had heard was the Promised Land—America. He described his trip to America as being pretty rough, on a cattle boat with accommodations not much better than those of the cattle. The boat was called the Sicilian Prince and sailed from Piraeus, Greece, on March 23, 1907, arriving in New York City on April 3. The ship's manifest indicates he owned the total sum of $35. Dad was processed through Ellis Island. Part of the process was to convert his name to English, and he was eventually registered as George Xenephon Vrilakas, although the ship's passenger manifest spelled his name "Vrilakis." One of his brothers (Antonio), who came to America later, found his name translated as Brilakis which is probably correct, as the surname of Greek natives of Crete traditionally end with "is." The letter V in the Greek alphabet could have easily been mistaken as a B.

My father never gave the details of this sudden change in his life, although he was reconciled with his father in later years. He never talked much about his life in Crete, but did tell us about, as a youngster, riding out to sea on the backs of giant turtles that came up on the beach. During the Turkish occupation of Crete, raids of Cretan's homes occurred occasionally and relations between the Cretans and Turks were less than friendly. At the age of twelve, my father was kidnapped by Turkish raiders and locked up in an abandoned building. He was fortunate that the raiders only took his shoes, locking him up so that they could make their escape. On another occasion my grandfather caught a Turk looting their home. A fight followed during which my father's oldest brother appeared on the scene and dispatched the looter with the threat of the family blunderbuss.

On arrival in New York City, my father found work in a cigar factory. Later he heard of better opportunities in Wisconsin and went there, possibly to Madison, to work in a candy factory. While there, and in pursuit of American citizenship, he enrolled in a class to learn to read and write English. He became even more interested in his teacher, May Topping of Delevan, Wisconsin. A courtship ensued, followed by their marriage in 1911.

May Topping was born on May 14, 1874, one of six children on a Wisconsin farm at a place later named Topping's Corner. Her ancestors appear to date back to a Sir Topping in England who reportedly fled religious persecution in England and immigrated to America. Somehow descendants ended up in Wisconsin where May's father, Jared Topping, farmed and sold farm equipment. May became a school teacher and met the young immigrant George in her English class.

May's parents were not very happy about their daughter suddenly marrying a Greek immigrant, who they felt couldn't support her in the manner to which she was accustomed. Under such circumstances my father and mother decided to make a life of their own, and answered the call to the west at that time. Shortly after their departure by train, they were intercepted by a police officer who advised them that May's father had requested they be apprehended and returned to Wisconsin. Mom told the officer she loved her husband, was travelling of her own free will, and wished to continue to California with him. The officer deferred to her desires.

They arrived in the Red Bluff area of Northern California, chosen because there had been a concentrated land advertising program in the east, offering land at bargain prices in the surrounding country. Able to speak only limited English, lacking funds, and with no particular qualification for a job, my father turned to what little he had learned in Greece about farming. Although slight of build, his strong work ethic and ability to do the work of several men in a day were essential to making a go of it in his new environment. He applied the proud, independent spirit of Crete; he strongly believed in earning his own way and would never buy anything on credit. When he needed anything he'd save up the money until he could pay for it in cash.

The land sales were not as advertised in the east, so he travelled the area by horse and buggy, testing the soil with a spade. He finally settled on buying a 40-acre parcel of land in the country, seven miles south of the town of Red Bluff. He was now a naturalized citizen, but some in the community displayed their resentment of a Greek foreigner. He ignored that type of treatment as he won their respect.

Coming to California to live must have presented quite a culture shock to my mother, as she had left family and friends in comfortable, developed, beautiful surroundings to live on an underdeveloped farm in the very sparsely settled grasslands of the northern Sacramento Valley. The nearest general store was three miles away, while the town of Red Bluff was seven miles distant, and had to be reached by horse and buggy over dirt roads, dusty in summer and muddy in the winter. Without electricity or inside plumbing it was a pretty Spartan life compared to today's standards. Mom too worked extremely hard doing ranch chores plus rearing her children, first John and Mark and later me. My sister Harriet was born after we had moved three miles to the village of Proberta.

Later Mom would say, "How I longed to see a tree." She told us stories of her childhood, such as skating on frozen lakes, her brothers mischievously skating across ice fishermen's lines, and about the beautiful woods of her native Wisconsin. She did not miss the cold of

Wisconsin winters, however. She loved the mountains of the west and could view Mt. Lassen in the Sierra Nevada Mountains to the east and the coast range mountains to the west.

Mother was a person who, to paraphrase Will Rogers, never met anyone she didn't like. She found something good about everyone, although maybe to different degrees. In turn, everyone loved her. She was always kind, generous, sympathetic, and considerate. She had a good sense of humor, loved music, nature, and reading. She also had a way of making people feel perfectly at ease with her. Her kindness and tolerance probably caused us children to take advantage of her to some degree, but she always had our greatest love and respect, and there was never any doubt that she had great love for her family. She would work tirelessly with us and encouraged us in our school studies. It was great to have a school teacher for a mom and a person with her patience to help us. One of my cousins in Wisconsin has repeated over and over how much Mom was adored by her students and all who knew her there. Many of them, in their 80s when I talked to them, remembered her fondly as their school teacher some 70 years back. I too thought highly of her. She was a major influence on me and my life, always supporting and encouraging when it was needed.

Mom had a very difficult time at my birth as she was near 40 years of age. Shortly thereafter her hair turned snow white, which gave her a distinguished appearance. Once when she was dressed up to go out we kids, thinking it a compliment, said, "Mom, you look just like George Washington." I'm not sure she felt complimented, but as always she took it in good grace.

Mom had a distinct fear of heights. During horse and buggy days when she'd ride in the family buggy to town, she would have Dad stop the buggy, and then she'd walk across the narrow bridge crossing a creek and have him pick her up on the other side. In later years when we occasionally drove up to Mt. Lassen by car, the steep cliffs along the road caused her great anxiety. We children would try to avoid sitting next to her because her reaction to looking down a steep canyon was unconsciously to pinch us on the legs. I can't think of a profession less likely to appeal to her than to be a pilot, which may explain why flying never seriously entered my mind until much later, as you will find in the coming chapters.

Chapter 2—"Urban" Life

Following my brothers John and Mark, I was born on the farm on October 28, 1918; I'm not sure if it was a doctor or midwife in attendance. Both Mom and I were not in the best of health, and the story goes that I was often kept on the oven door to the kitchen wood stove for warmth. (Thereby providing a handy source for an occasional dig from my older brothers that I was "half baked to begin with!") I contracted yellow jaundice soon after birth and there was some question about my survival for a while. Consequently I was the "runt" of the family, always underweight and slow to grow physically. The folks worried about me, and it seemed as if there was always some new, natural cure for me to try, ranging from sugar soaked with kerosene (for suspected worms) to various mineral and smelly sulfur waters—all vile tasting. Later in life, when I was forced to live off tinned Spam, powdered eggs, and canned Vienna sausages, I could think back on my childhood sulfur treatments and be consoled by remembering—it could be worse.

In 1921, my dad decided to pursue other means of making a living so moved us to the small hamlet of Proberta, some three miles east of the farm and on highway 99W. The village consisted of about fifteen families, a one-room schoolhouse, a general store with post office, and a car repair shop and service station. Our new home was on about five acres, which ran from the center of town to the extreme outer edge. The house (frame with cedar shake) had at one time been a small hotel or rooming house. It was quite large compared to the house on the farm and boasted four bedrooms, a parlor, kitchen, dining room, and bathroom—no indoor toilet for several more years as the house was served by a two-hole outdoor privy. It also boasted the luxury of electricity and indoor running water.

After living so austerely on the farm, Mom must have been overjoyed with the change. The five acres permitted Dad to continue limited farming and to work at a local alfalfa processing mill. Three years later he bought the local car repair shop and service station. He had absolutely no knowledge or experience in that line of work, but plunged in and grew with it as the automobile became more prolific. He had a natural mechanical aptitude which we all inherited. Brothers John and Mark were particularly adept, and John at age fourteen had earned a reputation as an excellent auto mechanic. He was always coming up with a better way to do things. For example, during his high school years he developed a device to automatically dim the lights on a car. The device sensed the light from an oncoming car and would react by dimming the headlights from high beam to low beam. A few years later the same device came out on some General Motors cars. He may have also invented the first recreational vehicle in the form of a trailer. Still in his teens, he developed a trailer with a small gas stove in it and two metal beds. The beds folded out over the edge of the unit for use then folded compactly back into the trailer for travel.

While dad worked on cars, Mom had also acquired a modern invention. She now had a hand-operated clothes-wringer which attached to a wash tub. The corrugated washboard remained for a few years more as the primary means of washing clothes.

My sister, Harriet, was born shortly after we moved to Proberta. After three boys she was a delight to us all and, since Mom was reaching her mid 40s, Harriet was the last child. Throughout her life, and particularly after the passage of our parents, Harriet would provide the cohesiveness that has held us together. There was much of Mom in the way Harriet raised her own family of four children.

My memory sharpens with the beginning of school. There was no kindergarten available, so at age six I was entered into the Proberta Grammar School, just two blocks distance from our house. John and Mark were already students there; Harriet started three years after I did. The school consisted of one large room that could be partitioned into two rooms by large folding doors in the center.

Proberta Grammar School, 1924. The author is on the far left.

There was one teacher and fourteen students ranging from the first to the eighth grade. We were all taught in one room, the grades generally separated by seat rows. It's hard to imagine now how the teacher managed under those conditions, but somehow it got done. Heat for the school was provided by a large, pot-bellied wood/coal stove located at one side of the room. A large, outdoor, hand-rung bell mounted between two telephone poles called us to classes. The older boys got the privilege of pulling the rope to ring the bell. At the first class of the day and after lunch when the bell was rung, we would line up outside the front door. The teacher would then play a recorded march, usually the "Stars and Stripes Forever," on a hand-cranked Victrola while we marched single-file into the schoolroom and to our assigned seats. The morning session was always preceded by the "Pledge of Allegiance" to the flag, a practice I recall clearly and that appears sadly missing in schools of today.

I was the only first grader so received quite a bit of attention from the teacher. It was always a bit damaging to my ego when in front of all the other classes she would put me on her lap to study.

At one time during my eight years of attendance the school grew to thirty-five pupils, but with redistricting it shrank back to about fifteen by my graduation time. Four of us graduated from the eighth grade in 1932. Six months later, Adolf Hitler was appointed chancellor of Germany, and Japan had taken a somewhat belligerent approach to the United States. Little did we know at the time how much those events would affect our lives in the future. Also not recognized was that we had lived a somewhat difficult life that prepared us for adversity and conditioned us to meet the rigors of military training and combat.

Chapter 3—Life in the 1920s and 1930s

As I started high school in the fall of 1932, the world around me was undergoing major changes. The most noticeable to us were the signs of industrialization. In Proberta, where horses and buggies far outnumbered cars at the time of my birth, the march of modern technology and industry was apparent in trains, cars, telephones, and movies. The shop added its first telephone in 1928. Dad was never convinced his voice could fully transmit in such a manner, so raised his voice commensurate with the distance the call had to travel. When in the mid twenties radios started to appear, Dad became a dealer for Atwater Kent. The first radios he sold were crystal sets with three dials and headphones. It required an antenna of fifty feet, usually stretched from building to building or pole to pole. The sets had to be precisely tuned to a station with the dials. People would often gather at the shop in the evenings to listen in wonder as he reached stations in San Francisco and sometimes as far away as Salt Lake City. One man in Proberta often stayed up all night with his set so that, when conditions were just right, he could receive Cincinnati—a feat considered somewhat miraculous in that early era of electronics.

The town of Gerber, three miles southeast of Proberta, had a movie theater, where black-and-white westerns would screen to piano accompaniment. Gerber was also a railroad center where train and track maintenance facilities plus a round house were located. Freight trains going north would have one or two extra steam engines added in Gerber, since the extra power was required to pull them over the Siskiyou Mountains into Oregon. The engines, the largest of which were called Malleys, seemed monstrous to us. We could hear them start from Gerber with widely spaced "huffs" and sometimes a series of "chugs" in rapid succession as the driving wheels slipped on the tracks. Gradually the train picked up momentum, and by the time it reached Proberta it had gained considerable speed, going by like a behemoth—with spewing steam, clanging bells, and gigantic churning driving wheels. The sound from a distance was always a good sleep inducer, and on many nights I would follow the sound of a train starting out from Gerber then fall fast asleep by the time it reached Proberta, even though Proberta always got a steam whistle at the crossing in the center of town. A Malley steam engine is now kept in the Smithsonian Museum where its sounds are very realistically reproduced.

The most amazing technology of all was the airplane. They were still rare then, and when one flew over town the entire populace watched with great awe and interest. The first passenger planes seen were Ford Trimotors. They were navigated purely by dead reckoning and landmarks in day time and at night by rotating strong light beacons spaced several miles apart across the country. Blind flying (on instruments) in weather conditions had not been developed.

One day two Army biplanes circled overhead, then descended toward a field and landed in a cloud of dust west of Proberta. The whole town drove out to see what was going on. Two leather-jacketed pilots in spats were working on the engine of one of the planes. They repaired it, spun the propeller, and flew off to the north—a successful forced landing and emergency repair in a grain field. To us they were the equivalent of something from outer space.

One of the older boys in town had a hobby of carving and assembling wooden model airplanes. Most were World War I models. He did an excellent job, and by trading marbles, tops, or whatever we could come up with, we could acquire one and then spend hours "flying" it.

When I was twelve, Mark and I attended an air show in Red Bluff. For a couple of dollars each, we took a ride in an open-cockpit biplane. We were strapped in side-by-side in the rear seat with one seat belt serving us both while the pilot did a series of dives and wingovers. There was a stress bar going across the cockpit, which we held onto for dear life. It scared the heck out of me! The possibility of flying an airplane was quite likely furthered from my imagination.

But if modernity was evident in the whistle of the trains and the drone of the Ford Trimotor, it didn't seem to have reached rural medicine—with nearly disastrous results for me.

Our local doctor had an office in Red Bluff and drove ten miles to Gerber to administer to railroad employees a couple of times each week. If we needed his service we would flag him down as he drove through Proberta. Doc Bailey had served as an Army doctor in World I and was a small, brusque man with a drill sergeant's bedside manner. He almost always dressed in a vested suit—usually reduced to shirt sleeves and vest. His visits were always accompanied by orders to everyone in sight.

He diagnosed my occasional periods of lack of energy in summertime as malaria, and I still recall him commanding Mom, in no uncertain terms, that she could "let a rattlesnake bite me, but not a mosquito." His remedy for pneumonia during a winter was to fully open all my bedroom windows. Somehow I recovered anyway. Just prior to graduation from high school I contracted measles. I suffered complications totally unrecognized by Doc Bailey, and when I returned to school I became swollen and felt awful. Doc Bailey ordered Mom to feed me lots of milk, eggs, and meat to build me up. A short time later it became evident that something serious (and beyond Doc Bailey's ability to correct) was wrong, so my folks took me to a different doctor. He was young and progressive and immediately gave me a series of tests, something Doc Bailey had not considered necessary. The tests showed my urine to be twenty percent blood, and my blood to be sixty percent deficient in red corpuscles. My condition was diagnosed as acute kidney infection resulting from the measles complications. The new doctor put me in the hospital immediately and on a strict no-protein diet, in other words, no meat, eggs, or milk. Over the next year I made a full recovery, but another week of Doc Bailey's home remedies may well have put me away for good.

Almost forty years later, during a routine Air Force physical examination, the problem diagnosed as "malaria" by Doc Bailey was accurately diagnosed as Mediterranean Anemia, or Thalassemia Minor. Ironically, it is thought to occur precisely because it offers its sufferers protection from malaria. In fairness to Doc Bailey, that condition was unheard of in his day, but he caused me to swallow a lot of quinine unnecessarily and take prescribed loads of iron pills, which are not helpful and possibly harmful for those with Mediterranean Anemia. Fortunately the problem seemed to leave during my teen years and I did not noticeably feel its effect thereafter.

The Great Depression following the crash of 1929 hit the Northern California area hard. Our family survived it better than most largely through hard work, my dad's home gardening, and doing with less. It left an indelible impression that had a lifetime effect. It bothers me now, in more affluent times, to see families that live extravagantly or waste food and clothing. I'm still not assured that another crash cannot occur, and I worry that those who have failed to provide for a "rainy day" will suffer as we did then. Unemployment was rampant and federal or local government assistance was extremely limited. Somehow people helped each other to make it through. At the same time people started migrating west from the drought areas of the Midwest. They came with all their belongings strapped to their rundown cars, sometimes with a goat riding on specially built running board racks. Many settled in the area and pulled themselves up by their bootstraps over the ensuing years—mostly through hard work. Most people raised as much of their own food as possible and many kept a cow to provide milk and butter. Very little was wasted. I recall a man departing in his car from the repair shop and as he neared the highway he accidentally ran over a chicken belonging to a widow that lived nearby. He stopped, backed up to the chicken, where, without getting out of his car, he scooped it up from the ground, popped it into his car and sped off—no doubt delighted that his next meal was assured.

One summer, at the height of the depression, Mark came up with the idea that he and I should contract to pick all of the figs at a nearby fig orchard. We would dry them, sack them, and ship them to a buyer in San Francisco. A fall-back plan was that if they couldn't be sold for a profit, he would feed them to some pigs that he was raising as a high school class project. We worked diligently all through the harvesting season and accumulated about a ton or more of figs. We made sure they were thoroughly dried by the sun and sacked them in fifty-pound burlap sacks. Mark then wrote to a broker in San Francisco who wrote back to say he would buy the figs at some three cents per pound F.O.B. San Francisco. We didn't know what F.O.B. meant, but on further investigation found that we would have to pay the freight to the destination. A quick check with the local rail freight agent revealed that the cost of shipping the figs was almost exactly as much per pound as the price quotation. The pigs got the figs, and we learned a valuable lesson in commerce.

I started high school in the fall of 1932. It was a big step for any of us from Proberta, going from a one-room schoolhouse to a school with almost 400 students. Red Bluff Union High School served an area covering roughly a radius of fifteen miles from that 3,000-person town. We were bused the seven miles up and back each day. The bus serving Proberta at that time was a 1924 White, a rambling old breezy bucket of bolts that moved at a top speed of 35 miles per hour and often broke down en route. It had hard rubber tires on the rear wheels and even harder seats, which made the ride much less than comfortable. The driver always had difficulty shifting it from one gear to another. There would be much clashing and grinding of gears between shifts, accompanied by growls and curses from the driver—not to mention derisive smart-mouthed remarks from the passengers, such as, "Grind me a pound while you're at it," or "Grind 'em 'til they fit!" Somehow despite its age and infirmity the bus stayed on the road for at least three of my four years of high school.

The freshman class at that time was always subject to some friendly hazing, and one day was set aside for that particular purpose. Freshmen anticipated that day with a certain amount of trepidation. One of the seniors, the town bully of Red Bluff and the spoiled son of a local banker, had made it his primary endeavor to live up to the reputation of being a general all-around jerk during his four years of high school. On the day of the freshman initiation we were called up on the auditorium stage one at a time, where we all got some kind of hazing, generally a painted face or something to make us look ridiculous. As I crossed the stage, the senior class bad boy threw me in a chair, put a barber's frock over me, and announced that I needed a haircut. Everyone thought it was being faked, although it felt pretty real as he wielded hand clippers and hair fell down around my face. Even so I still didn't believe it was happening. His instructions were for me to leave the stage and walk across the front row of the auditorium so that everyone could see how much better I looked!

I didn't get to witness the ensuing good part, but my brother Mark (who played first string football), having witnessed what happened and having had some prior unpleasant experiences with the guy, met him coming out into the hall with a couple of loaded fists. Quite a battle followed during which the bully may have learned more than he had learned in his previous three years of high school.

The principal was thoroughly distraught over the whole thing and told Mark later and privately that the bully had received what he very much deserved. He then called me in and had the bully formally apologize, a formality that seem to carry very little sincerity on the part of the bully. There were some positive results from the incident, however. Every student and teacher knew me after that and nobody gave Mark much sass.

High school opened new vistas for me. It was great making so many new friends and expanding my social life beyond the confines of Proberta. I also began to develop more physically, although not a great lot. My weight was 97 pounds at the start and about 120 at graduation.

Mark and John had both been good athletes in high school before me, John as a broad jumper in track and Mark excelled in both football and track. I must have been a disappointment to the athletics coach but did play basketball with the "D" team, for those under 125 pounds. Practice took place in the morning before classes started, which meant the three of us from Proberta arose in the dark at about 5:30 a.m., made breakfast on a wood stove, hitch-hiked the seven miles to Red Bluff, then walked a mile to the high school gym. We would often be so cold when we got there our fingers were too numb to handle the basketball. It made for a long day, but seemed most worthwhile at the time.

I can now appreciate the fact that we had some wonderful, dedicated teachers in high school. One in particular was determined to drill as much knowledge of typing or shorthand into us as she could. She was also a strict disciplinarian when occasion demanded and could hurl a blackboard eraser the length of her classroom with unerring accuracy. I was in one of her typing classes and had the good fortune to sit next to Nettie Chew, an excellent student who always found time to explain anything to me again if I didn't get it the first time. Nettie could type 60 words a minute while doing her fingernails, while I, at best, could rap out 20 if I got my hands positioned properly to begin with and didn't get my fingers lodged in between the keys as I typed.

A feature of the typewriter of that era was a little bell that tinkled to signal the right margin and to tell us to manually return the carriage for the next line. We soon discovered a lever in the back of the typewriter that would ring the bell repeatedly when properly manipulated, something that was distracting to the class and that Mrs. Adams, understandably, did not appreciate or abide. One warm spring day Nettie was busy rattling out words at 60 per, while I sat idly looking out the window, probably dreaming of summer vacation, and absentmindedly triggering the bell on my typewriter. I was startled out of my reverie when something struck me square in the chest with a loud splat, and a white cloud of chalk dust arose over both Nettie and me. I looked up to an icy stare from Mrs. Adams, and it was obvious she wanted my attention back in the classroom. Nettie had speeded up to about 80 words per minute, and I immediately set a new record of 40. I've used my typing skill a lot during the years since then and will always be beholden to Mrs. Adams. I do think she had missed her calling, however. She could have been a star pitcher for the Boston Red Sox!

It wasn't just typing that remained with me after high school. The high school boys of Proberta formed a somewhat loosely organized club and we often gathered in an old shed behind the general store. The shed had electric lights and a stove for heat so we would sit around the stove some evenings swapping stories of the day. Smoking cigarettes was the "in" thing to do at that age and time, and we would occasionally share cigarettes with whoever might have come by a pack (usually filched from a parent). I had a penchant for cigars and the shed provided a great place to puff on a stogie, since smoking was not condoned by our parents. One night I had come by a cigar and was sitting among the club members enjoying it to the utmost. At about the halfway mark of the cigar, there was a knock on the door followed by its sudden opening—and I found myself enveloping a very surprised father with a neat smoke ring. He expressed his displeasure with my particular behavior, after which I extinguished the cigar, but not soon enough to avoid the nickname "Smoky" from the fellow members. The nickname became a fixture around high school and has remained with me ever since.

Following high school my parents encouraged me to go to junior college to study accounting and business administration. My first year was at Long Beach Junior College (now Long Beach City College) because John was there as an engineer on a prominent Los Angeles lawyer's yacht. We roomed together on Cedar Street in Long Beach. Long Beach was another big step toward urban life and it took some adjustments, such as how to identify the right bus to take to the campus and which side of the street to catch it on. By the next year John had moved to another location, so I transferred to Sacramento Junior College. Some Red Bluff High graduates were also attending there, so we saved on housing cost by joining up and renting an apartment.

After another year at Sacramento Junior College, I graduated in 1939 with an Associate of Arts degree. It wasn't enough really to be prepared for the business world, but after some searching I went to work as a bookkeeper for a Sacramento paper company. Pay was $65 per month, and I thoroughly disliked being confined in an office, trying to make figures balance. In about four months, an opportunity arose to work in a company-owned Union 76 gasoline service station. The offer was for almost double my salary plus commissions, so I took it.

After a short training session in Oakland, I was assigned to a new station in Corning, followed by a transfer to Red Bluff and finally to Redding. Having had considerable experience in my dad's garage and service station while growing up, the transition was easy, and although there didn't appear to be a great future in that business, it was financially rewarding, provided good sales experience, and paid for my ownership of a 1932 Model A Ford roadster.

In retrospect there was little need to be concerned about my future. It had been ordained without my knowledge of it. Rumblings around the world and events at that time ultimately lead me in an entirely unexpected and unpredictable direction for the rest of my life. Daily radio broadcasts and movie newsreels often featured Germany's Hitler ranting to enthusiastic audiences of thousands, all chanting Sieg Heil on cue. The possibility of America being embroiled in another war became the main topic of conversation on the street. There were rumblings of discord with Japan also, and as Hitler began his march into Northern and Western Europe, challenging Britain and France in the process, talk of compulsory military training for those 21 to 35 years of age became more and more prominent. In September 1940, as Jews in Germany were ordered to wear yellow stars, German bombers were bombing London, and Mussolini's Italian troops were spreading across North Africa, selective service became a reality.

We all registered for the draft and were classified according to our physical condition, marital status, and/or need, if employed in a defense-related industry. I was classified 1A in 1940, and knew then that it would be only a matter of time before my life would take a dramatic change, although at that point we didn't think seriously about war. We thought it was just a case of leaving civilian life for one year's training in the military.

My draft notice came up in the spring of 1941, while I was working at the gas station in Redding. I continued working at the station, but started making plans, such as disposal of my car and storage of my belongings with my parents. I felt sure that I was physically qualified to become a draftee and the 1A classification assured my being tapped. The Union 76 company notified me the company would continue paying two-thirds of my base pay for the first three months of my draft obligation, which was a nice gesture and a big boost to the $21 monthly pay of an army inductee at that time.

The Tehama County draft board directed me to report to the selective service board in Red Bluff on July 8, 1941, for induction into the army. I sold my beloved Model A Ford for $80 and joined about fifteen others from Tehama County reporting on that date as directed. We were then put on a bus to Sacramento, where we were given a physical and formally inducted into the Unites States Army. That same day we were bused to a reception center at Fort Ord. My military life had begun.

Chapter 4—Army Training

Within twenty-four hours, I was transformed from a service station attendant to an Army basic soldier in the United States Army at Fort Ord, Monterey.

Despite the midsummer heat, we were issued winter, olive-drab, wool uniforms. Even our underwear and socks were olive drab. None of the uniforms fit. Our first taste of army discipline was meted out by a very self-important young corporal who appeared periodically like a Napoleon at the end of the company street. He instructed us that when he blew his whistle, we were to fall out on the double in full dress. He did this all day and we never pleased him. The speed of light would not have been fast enough. A form of Army discipline had begun.

After a few days our names began to appear on shipping rosters, and before long I was ordered to basic infantry training at Camp Roberts, California, near the old mission town of San Miguel in the Salinas Valley. It was miserably hot there during my three-month stay. The wooden barracks never did cool down. Mobilization had begun, but at a slow pace, so the camp was poorly equipped in both experienced people and equipment. Basic infantry training is about ninety percent discipline and physical training, so we marched some twelve miles per day, practiced bayonet drill and close order drill, ran the obstacle course, and learned to fire the machine gun, pistol, and rifle. Most of the rifles were World War I Enfields, although the M-1 Girand later became standard equipment.

The area was loaded with tarantulas and rattlesnakes, so it wasn't uncommon to meet up with one or the other on field exercises. One day, while leading my squad along the Salinas River, I led them in a dive under a large bush for cover from the "enemy." A loud buzzing sound brought us immediately back out. We fixed bayonets and annihilated a five-button rattler on the spot. At another time I had dived to the ground during a practice infantry advance. Peeking up over my rifle to get the lay of the land, I noticed a large hairy object crawling across my line of vision about a foot ahead. It was a monstrous black tarantula trying to remove itself from the "war zone."

Camp Roberts, California

Private Robert Vrilakas
Camp Roberts
July 1941

If we didn't learn much about infantry tactics, we did get in good physical shape during the time at Camp Roberts. I found that size didn't make much difference. In fact anyone carrying extra personal weight either had to work it off or suffer, particularly on long marches with full field pack.

My squad at Camp Roberts, California, 1941

On Saturday morning we'd have barracks inspection and everything had to be shined and placed near our bunks in precise order. Our bed had to be made with the blanket stretched so tight a penny tossed on the surface would bounce. David Johnny, whom we all liked, was an American Indian from a tribe in Northern California. He could never master the bed making routine. So on Friday evenings we would help him make it up and he'd sleep on the floor next to it, all prepared to pass inspection the next morning. He often repaid the favor by helping to carry one's pack on hikes.

Our pay as a basic draftee was $21 per month. At payday we'd line up alphabetically by last name and proceed through a pay line. After deductions, we netted about $18 at the end of the line. A large craps game always took place in the barracks that night, sometimes by flashlight long after lights out and "Taps" had been sounded. If your bunk was on the first floor you could hear the "bones" rattling about on the floor above.

There were four of us from the Red Bluff area going through Camp Roberts training at the same time. One of the four had a Ford coupe with rumble seat, so on weekends when we didn't have a duty assignment we would pool our money for gasoline and leave for home immediately after Saturday morning inspection. It was a long trip, but we'd arrive home in time to attend an outdoor local dance hall, catch some sleep, a good home-cooked meal the next day, and then hurry back to camp to be there by two a.m. Monday—or sometimes just in time to beat the bugle sounding reveille at six a.m.

With basic training completed at Camp Roberts at the end of September, it was time to sweat out the next assignment. Mine was particularly desirable, as it turned out to be the 7th Infantry Division at Fort Ord, Monterey. This was a line outfit with a lot of history, so those of us assigned were proud to be a member. I was assigned to a heavy mortar company of the 32nd battalion. Part of my job was to carry the mortar base plate from one location to another. It weighed 40 pounds, and with a full field pack that meant carrying almost two-thirds of my body weight. Training for that was short lived, however, because about three weeks after my arrival I was told to report to battalion headquarters for duty as a clerk-typist. Someone had looked over my record and found that I could type and take shorthand. It was a disappointment to me because I had become accustomed to my initial assignment and liked those who were in the company.

My job at battalion headquarters was to process hardship discharges. Those who had a bona fide case with proof that their assignment to the Army caused a severe hardship to dependent parents could obtain an administrative discharge. Some of the applications were genuine tearjerkers with affidavits from parents, clergymen, and prominent acquaintances. Others were obvious attempts to get out of service, using the hardship route as a means. I'd gather all the documentation together, make copies, write and type a cover letter with space for approval or disapproval, then forward it all to higher headquarters for continued action.

I obtained an approved pass and was looking forward to spending Christmas at home. On December 7th while taking advantage of Sunday, the one day we were allowed to sleep in, the first sergeant burst into the open bay barracks at about 10:00 a.m. and announced that the Japanese had attacked Pearl Harbor, and a declaration of war was expected immediately from the president and Congress. All leaves and passes were cancelled. President Roosevelt, with Congressional approval, gave his famed "Day of Infamy" speech and declared war on both the European Axis and Japan at 4:00 p.m. the next day.

It was not necessary for the Division to immediately receive formal notice of war status, although that word arrived shortly thereafter. We were all a bit stunned and at a stage of not knowing what to expect next. Very soon, however, we were told to report immediately to the supply room to clean preservative grease from rifles, and that a Japanese attack on the West coast was very likely. After feverishly working on the rifles for several hours, we were ordered to get all of our military gear together and stand by to evacuate the fort. At this point everything was in a state of confusion, with wild rumors flying in all directions. There was genuine fear that the Japanese would attack. Units of the 7th Division were being dispersed up and down California for the purpose of guarding bridges, highways, and other possible sabotage points. Near dusk we were put on trucks and hauled out to the wooded area east of the fort where we were to set up pup tents and experience full field conditions, mess tent and all.

The first night we slept wherever we could find a spot to put down our blankets. Prohibited from turning on headlights, some of the trucks in the confusion ran over sleeping soldiers. We were told to be on constant alert for air attack and to keep under cover and concealment as much as possible. To add to our miseries it started to rain and turned cold. With all the vehicle traffic the entire area became a quagmire. We did our best to perform guard duty around the perimeter of our encampment and to improve living conditions. Everything was wet in my pup tent, and life got pretty miserable after a short time.

In a few days we were trucked back to our barracks where we hurriedly packed all of our civilian clothes in a duffel bag and put a shipping tag on it addressed to our respective homes. I never saw my bag or its contents again, but thought at the time how luxurious it would be if we could move back into those relatively warm, dry barracks. Over the next ten days, conditions improved somewhat and confusion lessened to some degree. We had some time on our hands and began to absorb the impact of how our lives had changed and to think about what might be expected in the future. It was clear that the more comfortable, stable life of a garrison soldier, as experienced at Fort Ord, was now out the window. During the long hours of guard duty there was lots of time to reflect on what had happened, where I was, and what the future might hold.

Happily, I was being returned to my infantry unit, but had serious reservations about how to perform as a combat soldier. I had been taught how to march, fire a rifle, and set up a pup tent, but it seemed to me that my training for actual warfare was extremely limited and I was woefully lacking in any real understanding of combat tactics. News accounts and theater news reels pictured a powerful German and Japanese military, well trained and experienced. It also appeared inevitable that the 7th Division would be directly involved in the conflict. It was the pride of the Army. No longer was it just a civic duty to put in a year in the Army— my future for an unknown time would be determined by the war and my participation in it. It was evident that my fate and future were to be in the hands of the Army for some time. We were reminded again that under no circumstances, to include death in the family, would anyone be given leave of absence and that we could not wear civilian clothing for the duration of the war. I felt as if a wall had been erected, barring me from my family, old friends, and from my past. I considered myself fortunate in one respect; I was not romantically involved at the time and would not be leaving a future wife to await my return.

After about two weeks of field duty, orders directed me to report for duty as a clerk typist with 7th Division headquarters then located in the San Jose Armory, so I packed up my gear and moved. Living conditions at the Armory were much improved, but the hours were long and we never saw the sun except when going to the mess for lunch. I wasn't happy about leaving my buddies again to become a paper shuffler at headquarters. Wild rumors continued to fly, but there was a noticeable improvement in order.

A colonel, the deputy G-4 (Logistics) was my boss. He was an older southern gentleman who worked very hard and long hours. He never learned to pronounce my name, but under the pressures of the time it didn't bother me; besides, at that time I felt that colonels were superhuman, who only spoke directly to God (and other colonels or above). In fact, following the practice of the old Army, an enlisted person did not address an officer directly with the word "you." For example, he or she would correctly say "if the colonel wishes" rather than "if you wish." That custom seemed to wear away as the conscripted and volunteer complement became predominant.

Having completed two years of college made me eligible to become an army aviation cadet, if I qualified. That program put you into the Army Air Corps and under about a ten-month flight training program. Upon successful completion you graduated as a rated pilot and commissioned 2nd lieutenant. Upon receiving the first notice from the Army Air Corps advising me of my eligibility to apply, I had dismissed it as being far beyond my ability. My thought at the time was, *Oh sure, me fly? While I'm at it I might as well swim across the Pacific Ocean!* In my view then, flying an airplane happened to only a few very fortunate and gifted individuals. It certainly was not intended to happen to farm boys from Proberta.

A second notice caused me to do more serious reasoning. Going through the war as a clerk typist was not at all to my liking. Even if flying was not for me, by applying I would at least be transferred to the Air Corp where, if flying was not my bag, there would be a possibility of becoming an aircraft mechanic. So in April 1942, I filled out an application, took it to the orderly room, and waited. In a couple of weeks notice came to the office acknowledging my eligibility for training as an Army Aviation Cadet. It required release from my present assignment, so with fingers crossed and probably a few silent prayers, I put it in the colonel's in-basket and sat waiting breathlessly in the outer office for the call. A half hour or more went by, then I heard a few snorts and throat clearings from the inner office followed by the usual summons of "Varalaaarkus," which was as close as he ever came to pronouncing my name. I reported, and his words were a somewhat incredulous, "What is this?" I think it was the first time he had ever really looked at me. After some discussion it was obvious he couldn't understand why anyone should want to leave the infantry for such an upstart outfit as the Air Corps. Finally he resignedly said, "Well, okay."

The colonel may have understood my feelings and desires, because sometime after my departure he managed to take over an infantry unit. Unfortunately, I learned years later that, he was killed while leading an attack against the Japanese on Attu in the Aleutian Islands.

My morale immediately soared, along with some trepidation about starting off in a new and unknown direction. A week or so later during which I continued on the job as a clerk-typist, I was directed to report to Moffett Field, a nearby Naval Air Station, for a physical. Following that, Army orders directed me to report to an Air Corps unit in San Francisco. To my great surprise and delight, the word there was that there would be a month's delay getting into the program and that I'd be put on furlough until called.

A soldier from Fort Ord with a 7th Division patch on his shoulder sleeve had been just ahead of me in the reporting line, and I heard him say his name was Mills. A Fred Mills ran the general store in Proberta and had often said to me, "Bob, you should look up my nephew, Joe Mills, who is stationed at Fort Ord." I had intended to do it, but the war had sent us in different directions. During a pause I asked him if he had an uncle in Proberta, California, expecting him to say, "Where's that?" Instead he looked surprised and said, "Why yes, as a matter of fact I do, my Uncle Fred." We became good friends thereafter as we entered the flight training program at the same time and went through pre-flight, primary, and basic flight training together. Later he married a girl from Gerber who I knew, and our families have been lifetime friends.

It was great to go home, and my parents were delighted. Mom fed me as if the Army never had. I was to report to an Air Corp reception center for further physicals and scholastic tests, one of which would be math, including algebra. It worried me as I'd never taken an algebra course. This was a chance to take a home crash course in it. Mom, who had taken algebra many years before, was a great help in guiding me through a self-study course. Her patience and teaching ability got me to where I needed to be.

By this time most of my age group had gone off to military service, so that made me a pretty eligible date around home. My social life thrived, and after a month passed a telegram arrived saying my furlough had been extended another thirty days, but to be available to report immediately if called. By this time I felt more like a civilian again than a soldier, but two weeks into the extension another telegram arrived directing me to report immediately to the aviation cadet reception and pre-flight center at Santa Ana, California.

It was difficult to say goodbye again, and even more difficult for my parents, not knowing when, or if, they would see me again. As a parent now, I can fully appreciate how they felt.

Chapter 5—Cadet Flight Training: PT-17, BT-13, AT-6, and AT-9

Preflight at Santa Ana meant starting all over again. Most of the cadets came directly out of civilian life. Having been a soldier before made no difference, as we were all lumped together and put through basic training again—this time the Air Corps way. The previous military training made it easier, at least for me; I knew about military customs, how to march, do close order drill, and understood military discipline. Cadet training was even more vigorous than basic infantry, however. We did a lot more body building and as officer candidates were required to meet higher standards in everything. A noticeable difference in the official view of us was the improved food and living conditions.

The physicals and scholastic tests were something we all sweated out. Some didn't make it and were transferred out. One cadet in my section had been a professional baseball player. He was in excellent physical condition and we all envied his apparent potential for handling the cadet training program with ease. One day my training group was sent over to the infirmary for a blood test. Blood samples were taken from a vein in your arm, sometimes not too gently, and since fainting was an automatic wash-out, I was concerned about that. I'd seen some pretty hardy-looking individuals pass out before from that and immunization shots. The baseball player was showing off a bit after his blood sample by allowing a trickle of blood to run down his arm then wiping it back up with the cotton compress he had been furnished. I walked over to an open window, took some deep breaths, and tried not to think or watch what he was doing. Shortly there was a loud thud and there on the floor behind me was the baseball player—out like a light. He was revived and transferred immediately. The last we heard of him he had been assigned to the camp special services unit as an athletic instructor, his future as a military pilot and commissioned officer gone.

The people in the program stood out. They were all volunteers, had survived the rigors of the Great Depression, and were highly qualified physically and academically. Some were in their teens when they applied, but matured rapidly during their training regimen. A common characteristic of them all was that they were extremely eager to fly, and they were dedicated to the program. I felt that I would have to perform at the very best of my ability to keep up with them. To wash out was to most a fate worse than anything imaginable. Wash-outs did occur though, frequently and for a variety of reasons. Throughout the program we all, in the back of our minds, had the gnawing fear of not making it. That anxiety was with us night and day until we were commissioned. (Then we had other anxieties.) As aviation cadets we received $75 per month, so this was a big jump from previous military pay. Basic training was rigorous, and I don't think I've ever been in better physical condition.

After about six weeks we were transferred from Santa Ana to various primary flying schools. The time had come to bite the bullet and find out if we really could fly an airplane to military requirements. My assignment was to the Cal-Aero flying school near Ontario, California. It had been a commercial pilot training school prior to the war and operated on a contract basis to the Army during the war. The Army provided the school commandant and Army check pilots, but the instructors were all civilian. A typical day consisted of ground school for half the day, the other half being devoted to flight training. There would always be studies to keep us occupied at night and somehow or other calisthenics were squeezed in during the day. A page or two had been taken out of the West Point academy training. We were put under the honor system. As potential commissioned officers our word was our bond, a system that worked fine for those who could handle it. For those who couldn't, or abused it, it cost them their military flying careers. We were disciplined for minor infractions by being assessed points which had to be walked off on the aircraft ramp with a parachute strapped on our back. No passes were allowed to a cadet who had not walked off his assessed points.

We were assigned class number 43C as we entered. The class of

43B was our upper class who practiced hazing through the early part of the primary training phase. The hazing meant that we were required to spread our arms at every street corner and then, with arms ridiculously outstretched like wings, look right and left—clearing oneself—as one must do when flying. Having accomplished that successfully, one could then proceed around the corner. Our meals were called "square meals:" Food had to be picked up on a fork or spoon, moved straight out to about arm's length, then straight up until even with the mouth, then straight to the mouth. Swallowing it must have completed the square! Talking at the table was strictly forbidden except to ask another cadet to pass something. At night, about once a week, some upper classmen would come to our rooms, call us to attention and have us do various things, generally of a humorous nature, without smiling. A smile would bring an order to "wipe it off, throw it on the floor, step on it, put it in a wastebasket, and carry it outside." Fortunately as time went by and our schedule of work increased the hazing decreased considerably.

Ground training consisted of classes in navigation, weather, aerodynamics, and engine mechanics, to include hydraulics, electronics, and various aircraft systems. Flight training was accomplished in an Army designated PT-17 (Primary Trainer). It was a Stearman with two open tandem-seated cockpits and with two sets of controls. The fabric-covered biplane was equipped with a 225-horsepower radial engine.

The engine was started by an inertial flywheel which was hand cranked up to speed by a ground crewman, then engaged after making sure the propeller was clear and the pilot loudly calling out "CONTACT." Cockpit instruments consisted of air speed indicator, altimeter, magnetic compass, and a few engine-monitoring gauges. The PT-17 had a rugged exterior with a skid under the tail and narrow-based front wheels. The closely spaced landing gear made it susceptible to ground loop under a crosswind when landing—that is go into a sudden uncontrolled 360-degree turn on landing rollout, causing a wing to drag. It was nicknamed "The Yellow Peril," not because they were necessarily dangerous, or painted yellow, but because they were a peril when flown by cadets! The instructor occupied the front seat and talked to the student through a gosport (a hollow tube with a kind of funnel at the speakers end). The gosport tube was attached at the other end to the student's cloth helmet, carrying the instructor's voice much in the way that a doctor's stethoscope works. There was no tube going back to the instructor—no doubt based on the premise that a cadet couldn't possibly have anything of importance to say. Some instructors (fortunately not mine) used it as an instrument for punishing a particularly slow-learning cadet by holding the mouthpiece out in the wind stream in flight.

PT-17, with open cockpits in tandem, Cal-Aero Field, 1942.
Stearman's fabric-covered biplane provided the author
with his first pilot training experience and solo flight.

My civilian instructor was a mild-mannered, patient person, very dedicated to teaching his five assigned students how to fly. The first time we flew with him was greeted with great anticipation, because we didn't know whether we'd be sick, scared out of our wits, or what to expect. The first flight consisted of the instructor flying around the local area, demonstrating the function of the joy stick, ailerons, elevator, rudder, and what happened in a stall. He demonstrated climbs, dives, and the need for coordinating rudder and stick, always emphasizing the need to keep one's head out of the cockpit and eyes on the lookout for other aircraft.

Primary instructor and students.
Front row, left to right: Mork, intructor Moore, Mills;
Back row, left to right: Vrilakas, Archer, Hardison. 1942

Primary flight
training in PT-17
with
instructor in front,
author in back.

Some students did get air sick and a few decided they couldn't hack flying, but generally everyone liked it and was eager to continue their training. If you became airsick on any flight (fortunately it never happened to me), your first job after landing was to get a bucket of water and wash down the airplane. One cadet in my fivesome washed his aircraft after at least a dozen flights before being eliminated from flight training.

Like so many other things, flying turned out to be much less difficult than I had anticipated, and I became more confident that it was within my realm with every flight. I found that my inherited mechanical aptitude and limited experience in mechanics helped a great deal. You had to have a feel for how the engine was performing, as well as for other mechanical components of the aircraft.

Flying took me into another world. At that time it was a somewhat unexplored world, experienced by relatively few people. It was a world of great wonders and an entirely different perspective of the environment we lived in. Sometimes it was charged with thrills and excitement. Sometimes it could turn downright dangerous and scary, but it had a great fascination that drew you back to it. For better or worse, I was hooked, and soon began to look forward to every scheduled flight.

After about eight hours of instruction in the air and countless hours of ground school, the instructor took his five students to an auxiliary grass-covered field near Ontario. He had me shoot a couple of landings, then taxi over to the parking area where he climbed out and said, "Okay, you're on your own. Shoot a couple of landings and then come in and park it."

It was the big moment. Every pilot can remember every detail vividly and describe his feelings about his first solo flight. Flying with an instructor who was always there to take over the controls and "save you" in a landing or air maneuver was one thing. To have that reassuring crutch suddenly removed was like being thrown into the middle of an ocean full of sharks. It felt absolutely devastating at the time.

I conjured up what I hoped was a confident look and taxied away between feelings of high exultation and deep misgivings—and all the time trying to remember and do everything just as the instructor had taught me. A light from the control tower provided traffic control since the PT-17 had no radios. After checking magnetos and controls at the end of the dirt runway, I looked at the tower and noted the green light clearing me for takeoff. The moment of truth had arrived, and with much the same feeling as diving off a 150-foot tower into a small tank of water, I released the brakes and started advancing the throttle. Takeoff proceeded uneventfully. I found myself all alone in the air and wondering if this could all be true. Everything went well around the traffic pattern, and as I lined up and throttled back for approach to the runway, a reassuring green light clearing me to land flashed from the tower. I had relived my entire life during that trip around the field.

A fence at the end of the field made it necessary to clear that but still get down within the confines of the air patch. Everything was going quite smoothly as I set up a glide path and maintained final approach speed. Landings, of course, were the most difficult part of flying the PT-17, particularly in a crosswind. The landing required leveling off just above stall speed with the wheels just off the ground and the airplane in a three-point landing position. Front wheels and tail skid should touch the ground just at the point of stall. For reasons I still can't explain I left most of the final part of that procedure out and hit the ground pretty much at my glide attitude. The result of that was a ricochet back into the air to an altitude of about fifty feet. To make matters worse, the plane went into a vertical left bank. I looked down the left wing and saw it narrowly missing the ground. When you have been trained enough in a particular emergency, certain procedures seem to shout at you when needed. The instructor's often-repeated words to hit the throttle and go around when in trouble on landing made it almost an automatic reaction. So with full power I managed to level the wings, just as the aircraft skimmed back along the ground, climbed slowly and safely out of trouble, and headed around the pattern again, much embarrassed by my performance. My concern at that point was what the instructor might be thinking. Would he wash me out? Was flying, which I had learned to love, no longer going to be available to me? This landing had better be a good one! It was, but

I landed at the far edge of the runway which was over an incline and out of view of my instructor. He wasn't sure whether I had landed or crashed until with great relief he saw me taxiing over the hill into view. He met me at the plane and said quietly, "That will be all for today." The other cadets later said he had started toward me on the first landing attempt and had inadvertently pulled the "D" ring on his parachute, which he had in hand, leaving the canopy trailing out behind him.

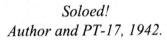

Soloed!
Author and PT-17, 1942.

Having soloed, the rest of primary flight training consisted of more dual rides with the instructor, plus continued ground school and solo flights. We learned to do loops, spins, snap rolls, pylon eights, Immelmams, and a dozen other maneuvers to improve flight proficiency and coordination. I may have taught myself a lesson about final approach and landing as the problem experienced on my first attempt never reoccurred. There were some ground loops and close calls by various cadets. My roommate landed one day, and while on landing roll another cadet landed on the tail of his aircraft. The propeller of the second aircraft took large gouges out of the fuselage of the first, finally coming to a stop as it cut into the parachute on my roommate's back. Both survived without injury, but the cadet in the second aircraft was immediately washed out.

At the end of about 80 flying hours and 60 days, we were given a check ride by an Army check pilot and were then ready to advance to basic flight training.

Class book picture of author at completion of primary flight training at Cal-Aero Field. Note gosport attachments on helmet.

This meant a change of station and a different airplane, so I received orders transferring me to Lancaster, California, in the Mohave Desert. The facility there was also a former civilian pilot training school, now under contract to the Army.

We were taught to fly the BT-13 (Basic Trainer). It had a metal external covering except for control surfaces and was a low-wing plane with two tandem seats and a Plexiglas canopy covering the cockpits. Manufactured by Vultee Aircraft Company, it had earned the nickname of "Vultee Vibrator." The radial engine, in the area of 425 horsepower, shook the entire aircraft. The metal wings also tended to flex and wrinkle under any stress. In a spin the sound reminded one of sheet metal flapping in the wind. The BT-13 had a variable pitch propeller (a first for us) and sounded like an angry bee on takeoff when the prop was maintained at low pitch. Heavier and with more torque, its stall characteristics were more pronounced and it was less forgiving than the primary trainer in a stall or spin. There was a trade-off, of course: the BT-13 had more speed and two-way radio communication. No more gosports—the instructor could now converse with us by intercom and we could respond.

After soloing in the BT-13 we were introduced to night flying and formation. Calisthenics and ground school continued along with general military training. Formation flying encompasses a whole new set of techniques and use of the controls in flying. It requires good judgment of speed relative to other aircraft plus acute depth perception. Some found it very difficult. Fortunately I adapted to it easily and enjoyed flying on the wing of another or leading a flight.

The desert environment at first seemed desolate and uninteresting, but by the end of our training at Lancaster it had grown on me, and I found it interesting. There is much more than meets the eye behind the sage brush and cactus in the form of plant and animal life. The pristine air that could be lacking in an urban area was always prevalent on the desert. People who lived on the desert obviously enjoyed living there despite the searing heat in the summer time. Now air conditioning has improved that matter considerably. The town of Lancaster looked like something out of an old Western movie with board sidewalks, dirt streets, and a saloon or two.

Occasionally we would be "buzzed" by P-38 pilots from Muroc Air Base (now Edwards Air Force Base). They would come skimming in over the desert at very high speed, leaving us totally in awe as they pulled straight up in a climb to several thousand feet, almost disappearing from view. It was an incredible sight and always left me with the thought that to fly them someday would be the height of my dreams.

Basic flight training finally ended and roughly half of the class was assigned to advanced training in single-engine aircraft, which pointed toward ultimately becoming a fighter pilot. The others were assigned to twin-engine schools, thereby being destined to fly multi-engine bombers or transports. My assignment to Luke Air Base, Arizona, for single engine training was exactly what I had hoped for. Advanced training was the final phase and, if successfully completed, would be climaxed by graduation from the cadet program, a pilot rating, being commissioned as 2nd lieutenant, and hopefully the opportunity to fly the latest in military aircraft.

The advanced trainer AT-6 which we were to fly was a dream compared to the BT-13.

Author in AT-6 (Advanced Trainer), Luke Air Base, 1943.

Manufactured by North American Aviation, it was fast for a trainer, had retractable landing gear, hydraulic flaps, and a dozen other features we had not experienced before. It was comparatively quiet in flight, very maneuverable and an excellent all around trainer. It also had a 30-caliber machine guns (mounted in the wing) for aerial and ground gunnery. Except for less engine power, it approached some of the earlier fighters of those years; in fact it resembled a P-36 which had been one of the Air Corps' front line fighters until about 1940.

Our training, now entirely by military pilot instructors, encompassed a number of things we had not experienced before, such as air-to-air and air-to-ground gunnery, instrument flying, etc. For safety reasons we were officially restricted from doing much aerobatics or dog-fighting when solo, but we would sometimes sneak over behind the nearby White Tank Mountains and have at it, until an instructor would show up and run us all out of the area.

My instructor was a young 2nd lieutenant from about three classes ahead of me. He was conscientious and thorough. One day he showed me a trick of slipping the plane sideways in one direction or the other by applying a rudder while holding the wings level. He said if you were ever being shot at from behind by another aircraft and couldn't shake him off your tail, this could cause him to miss because your aircraft would be slipping out of its apparent line of flight. That little bit of advice was to save my life later.

About midway through advanced flight training a notice appeared on the bulletin board asking for eighty volunteers to fly P-38s after graduation. (Actually we would be required to fly whatever the Army directed us to fly, but no doubt this procedure got those who really wanted to fly a particular aircraft into a specific program). The P-38 was considered the Air Corps' best high-performance aircraft at that point, and I quickly signed up. Unknown to the signers we became part of a highly-classified plan to replenish certain P-38 combat units overseas with much needed replacement pilots. Now I just had to prove to my instructor that I could do it.

The AT-6 had two front landing wheels fairly close together and a tail wheel that, although fixed in a slot, could swivel when enough pressure was applied to it. These features produced a tendency, similar to the PT-17, for the aircraft to ground loop following a crosswind landing. Upon runway touchdown and as the plane continued down the runway decelerating in speed, the pressure of a crosswind had the effect of causing the plane to want to "weather vane" into the crosswind. This had to be overcome by proper application of rudder and brake on the downwind side. Not too difficult, depending on the speed and direction of the crosswind. I had flown three hours one day and was then scheduled for a night flight. After about two hours of night flight I came in for a landing. I noted a slight crosswind, and corrected for it on approach. All went well on my landing but upon relaxing a bit on the landing roll-out, a gust from the crosswind caused the plane to take a sudden lurch toward the edge of the runway. Despite my best efforts the tail wheel unlocked, throwing the aircraft into a 360-degree ground loop, lightly touching a wing in the process. Ground loops are just embarrassing, as they generally cause minimum damage to the aircraft and the strapped-in pilot may not experience any injury other than a possible thump on the side of the head from being hurled against the cockpit interior by centrifugal force.

It was a dreaded occurrence because, if negligence was determined to be a primary factor, elimination from the program at that stage of the game was still possible. Accident board proceedings always follow such an event, so I was directed to write a report of the accident. I had a contributing cause that I was aware of, but another that never entered my mind while writing the report. My 5-foot-8-inch height made it difficult for me to fully reach and operate the rudder and brake pedals in the AT-6, so I always used two back pads to offset that problem. On that flight I could only find one, and not wanting to miss my scheduled takeoff, decided to go with what was available. During the incident, I had been unable to fully reach and apply sufficient brake and rudder to prevent the tail wheel from disengaging. That however would not carry much weight with the board. In the final analysis it is the pilot's responsibility to take whatever means necessary to avoid an accident. Most aircraft accidents are, after investigation, chalked up as just plain "Pilot Error." At the end of my report, for no particular reason at the time, I noted that the accident had occurred after more than five hours of day and night flying. I don't think I slept a wink that night.

The next day the operations officer called me to his office. He seemed much more understanding than I had expected him to be and after some discussion came to the point. He said, "Look, your record has been good, but we're in a bit of a bind on this. There is a directive from higher headquarters that says we are, for safety reasons, not to fly a cadet more than four hours per day, unless an instructor accompanies him after that time. Somehow we mistakenly scheduled you solo beyond the four-hour limitation. Now I can get you through this with the board, but you will have to withdraw that part of your report relating to the number of hours you flew that day."

I had been totally unaware of any limitation on flying hours per day. It meant the operations officer was trying to save his own skin and was willing to save mine in the process (a quid pro quo so to speak). It felt like being thrown a lifesaver just before going down for the third time. I quickly agreed, and he, just as quickly, had a revised report typed up for me to sign. He then said, "Okay, now you have to appear before the accident investigation board tomorrow. Don't say anything except 'Yes, sir' and 'No, sir' to the board and I'll handle the rest." I met the board with a great amount of trepidation the next day, but everything went exactly as the operations officer had said it would. There was one heck of a relieved cadet back in the flying program practicing the old Army adage of keeping the mouth shut and the eyes and ears open, as well as an emphatic lesson about applying flight safety.

A highlight of advanced training was air and ground gunnery. We were sent down in small groups to Ajo, Arizona, on the Mexico border where we learned aerial gunnery by firing at a sleeve towed behind another aircraft. We also practiced air-to-ground gunnery by diving and firing on a ground target. It was miserably hot there, with abominable living conditions, but we didn't mind. One cadet in my group flew off into Mexico, got lost, and after running out of fuel, crash landed in the mesquite. He came back, looking very embarrassed, on a burro led by a Mexican man.

A week or so before graduation those of us who had volunteered to fly P-38s were sent to Williams Air Base nearby to check out in twin engine AT-9s. The plane was a two-engine trainer for future multi-engine pilots and was to provide us experience in twin-engine operation in preparation for check out in the twin-engine P-38. I was assigned to a hard-nosed 1st lieutenant instructor who practiced badgering his students unmercifully. To make matters worse he was scheduled for a leave, but had to check three of us out before he could go. This brought out more pressure and badgering from him, neither of which I responded to very well. Nothing seemed to go right until finally he said in desperation, "Go fly the damn thing even if you kill yourself in the process." I guess he figured the co-pilot would save me. I had had trouble making good landings in the AT-9, but without the instructor in the airplane everything went beautifully and my landings were all grease jobs. He couldn't have been anywhere near as happy to go on leave as I was to see him go, and thereafter I felt very much at home in the AT-9.

Back at Luke Air Base on March 10, 1943, the big day had finally arrived. We had completed our pilot training. We were designated aeronautical-rated pilots by Army order and commissioned as 2nd lieutenants. It was a great day of relief for all of us. We'd been through a highly-accelerated, rigorous training program for a period of almost ten months. The daily routine, with its constant stress and long working hours, caused several to fall along the way. As brand new 2nd lieutenants, now in officer's uniforms, we felt as if we had stepped into another world, and in many ways, we had. I had come further than I had ever expected, entering both the new world of flying and the Army Officer Corps, feeling confident and eager to fly a first-line fighter plane. It had been an arduous climb and reaching the goal had to compare somewhat with the feelings of those who reach the top of Mt. Everest. Although the remainder of my military career was as a commissioned officer, I was always glad that I had had enlisted experience. It gave me a perspective that was useful in command and staff positions. I never lost respect for the job that support and ground troops face, nor the fact that they are the backbone of the military.

Newly-commissioned 2nd Lt. Vrilakas, graduate of the aviation cadet program with Class 43C, Luke Field, Arizona, March 10, 1943.

There were telegrams of congratulation from old friends and the folks at home who had followed my progress and had been made aware of my graduation date. We were then off to our next assignment. Two men in our graduating Class of 43C at Luke Air Base would become famous. Chuck Yeager, several years later, became the first human to break the speed of sound. Dick Catledge, a standout in our class, later organized and led the first Air Force "Thunderbird" demonstration flight team. He was a member of the P-38 volunteer group, and we were later assigned to the same P-38 Fighter Group overseas.

Chapter 6—P-38 Checkout

Dick Lee appeared in my life as I settled in at Luke Army Air Base for Advanced Flight Training. He was assigned the bunk and living space next to mine in the barracks. Only about five feet six inches tall, he was a dynamic and at times a feisty individual. He had a good sense of humor, but was a no-nonsense person about flying. He also was of a genuine nature, never given to pretentiousness and intolerant of those who were. We became good friends, and I admired him as a person as well as a natural-born pilot. Learning to fly appeared to be second nature to him.

As we became more acquainted it was obvious that Dick had the markings of a classic fighter pilot. He loved flying and took to it like a duck to water. When he wasn't flying he was talking about it. As a pilot he was aggressive, eager, and had all the "right stuff" as attributed to some of the more publicized fighter pilots. We remained together on our assignments and during much of our flying for the next year. He became an ace, destroying five enemy aircraft in the air during our combat tour together, and after the war flew commercially over thirty years for TWA. He was a lifetime and very close friend, and I was much saddened by his passing away a few years back.

When the notice went up on the bulletin board at Luke Field, Arizona, asking for 80 volunteers to fly P-38s after graduation as 2nd lieutenants, Dick and I had both signed up. The list had filled quickly. There was always a certain amount of uncertainty connected with volunteering for anything in the Army, but the possibility of flying P-38s met our fondest desire.

True to the Army's word, following graduation on March 10, 1943, eighty of the graduating class who had volunteered for P-38s were shipped to the Lockheed plant at Glendale, California. There we were briefed by a colonel who told us we would be going to Muroc Dry Lake for check out in P-38s. Following that we were to be split up into three different operational training groups for further combat training. He said we were a select group destined for some highly interesting flying, but for security reasons he could not give us further details.

Muroc Air Base was a perfect place to fly out of. It had a fairly long runway centered on the bed of a dry lake. There were no obstacles around the base and the dry lakebed provided excellent terrain for a forced landing, if required. The desert surrounding it was practically uninhabited by people and there was a lot of airspace available. The downside of excellent flying conditions was that living conditions were a bit primitive. Tar-paper shacks provided our living quarters and other buildings. They were hot and uncomfortable, but we were much too busy to notice.

The P-38 was an awesome sight to us. It was at that time the Air Corps' top high-performance, high-altitude fighter. It was unique because of its speed and versatility, and it played a major role in World War II. It was, and still is, instantly recognizable from its two engines and twin-tail, twin-boom configuration, with the booms connected by the wing, the cockpit up front, and the horizontal stabilizer at the rear. The P-38 was rather large and heavy for a fighter of that day (approximately 15,000 pounds), but with its two in-line, liquid-cooled, 1,450-horsepower supercharged engines, it had much more power than other fighters. Four 50-caliber machine guns plus a 20-millimeter cannon all centered in the nose of the cockpit provided tremendous, concentrated firepower. In addition to its capability to reach high altitudes, it was a very stable platform for strafing ground targets or dive bombing.

Like all high-performance aircraft it had some characteristics that were less than desirable. To the inexperienced it was difficult to fly following the loss of an engine in flight. Until later models were developed with dive brakes it had a tendency to lose elevator control in a high-speed dive, because air passing over the wing would begin to burble and blank out the rear elevator, making it difficult or impossible at times to pull out of a steep dive. It also presented problems for bail out at certain speeds because of the position of the rear horizontal stabilizer. At low speeds the pilot could drop off the wing and exit below the stabilizer. At very high speeds some pilots exited over the top of it. In between those speeds there was a distinct possibility of being struck by the stabilizer. If sufficient control and optimum airspeed were available at bailout, the best procedure was to roll it on its back and drop free.

We were put right to work checking out. First we went to ground school classes where all the various systems on the aircraft were explained, usually by a Lockheed representative. We also spent hours sitting in the cockpit getting familiar with the location of all the instruments and controls. We'd sit in the cockpit of a P-38 and "play" like we had started the engines, taxied out, and took off. Finally we had to draw, from memory, a picture of the instrument panel showing the location of each instrument. Just before solo checkout we were given a short "piggy back" ride in a P-38 that had most of the radios removed from behind the pilot seat. Removal of the radios permitted just enough room behind the pilot for the student pilot to squeeze in and observe how things were done on an actual flight. We came down from the flight cramped but very much impressed by the speed and performance of the aircraft.

Although it was difficult maintaining brake pressure as I taxied out for my first solo flight, by the time I'd became airborne, I started to shake off much of my anxiety about flying the plane. I flew around a while getting the feel of it, and after practicing turns and stalls, went through an engine shut down and feathering procedure. It was a bit of a shock at 6,000 feet of elevation and 180 miles per hour to look out the cockpit to see the propeller on the dead engine sitting stock still. Until rudder trim was applied it required significant pressure on the side of the good engine to offset the asymmetrical power, but it was a great confidence builder as the airplane continued to fly beautifully. It could fly very well on one engine, but there wasn't much room for error if your engine shut down and feathering procedures were faulty.

My instructions were, after getting the feel of the aircraft, to set up a landing pattern at 6,000 feet, and with gear and flaps down practice setting up a pattern and approach speed with flare out and stall at 5,000 feet as if landing on a runway. The shut down engine unfeathered and started just as the book had said it would, so after several simulated landings it was time to return to Muroc for the real thing. Everything went well and despite the unfamiliar high approach and landing speed it settled smoothly on the runway. Back at the parking space, with legs again about to surrender from constantly working the brakes pedals, I shut it down and climbed out of what was then the Air Corps hottest fighter plane—about as proud of anything I'd ever done. As with most P-38 pilots, it was the beginning of an endless love affair.

Muroc was a lonely outpost in the desert, so since Dick Lee had obtained an old 1937 Ford V8, we would head for Hollywood on weekends. The Biltmore Hotel was the gathering place for cadets and flying officers, and we would trade yarns on flying experiences, the cadets looking up to us much as if we were from outer space. The Biltmore Hotel catered to us, and we enjoyed the luxury of a good shower and comfortable room for a night in contrast to the austere surroundings of the barracks at Muroc Air Base. Hollywood was somewhat subdued, as all cities were during the war, but it was an exciting place to visit for a person not used to much more than a church festival in Proberta. We did not have time to take in the sights of Hollywood, but it was a great place to belly up to the "watering hole" and trade experiences with other newbie pilots from the Navy and Marine Corps. We also enjoyed a good Hollywood restaurant dinner on occasion, usually a steak with all the trimmings. If we saw any movie stars we did not recognize them. The renowned Hollywood Palladium was in full swing at that time, and we would, on occasion, get to attend some of the top bands of the day playing for our listening and dancing enjoyment.

We'd unwind over the weekend, and then travel half the night to get back for Monday morning operations. Because of gas rationing for automobiles, having enough fuel to get back and forth was a problem.

We solved that very neatly by drawing it from the drain cocks of a P-38 on the ramp. The gasoline was about 110-octane and no doubt didn't do Dick's Ford engine any good, but it got us back and forth.

One night on our way back I was asleep on the back seat when we suddenly stopped and I was awakened by a highway patrolman's flashlight. He was giving Dick a lecture for doing 90 mph and said, "I'm getting damn tired of chasing you pilots who think you should fly on the ground." There was no ticket though, just the lecture.

We kept building up flying time and were beginning to feel more like we had control of the aircraft than vice versa. P-38s were unique because of the counter rotating props, which at equal power settings eliminated the torque problem experienced in single-engine planes. We did not have to constantly apply rudder to compensate for speed or torque, so it was possible to pull straight up in a climb until the airspeed indicator fell well below stalling speed. Instead of snapping into a spin condition, as a single engine aircraft would do, the P-38 would slowly fall into an attitude that would let it fly smoothly out of the stall condition.

Of course if you lost an engine you had an entirely different situation. You then had a great amount of torque plus the asymmetrical pull of the good engine offset from the center of the aircraft. If the aircraft stalled and was improperly handled, a violent spin was inevitable. It was a must that we practice single-engine operation on almost every flight. Occasionally we'd wheel over my old basic school at Lancaster to give the cadets a look at what a "real" airplane could do, remembering in the process how, not long before, we had been the ones marveling at the P-38's performance and wondering if we'd ever make it through cadet flight training.

On run up the P-38 put out a tremendous amount of prop wash, which was demonstrated to me dramatically while walking along the flight line one day. Someone had pulled up along the edge of the ramp in a P-38, turned the tail out away from other airplanes, and started a power check. What the pilot had not noticed was that the tail of the aircraft was pointed directly at one of the "one-holer" portable toilets that had been set up off the paved area. As he advanced power the building begin to shake violently and rock in various directions as if it were about to become airborne. At that moment the door flew open and someone with pants at half mast and a look of wild-eyed horror made a do-or-die-dash for safety. A few seconds later the outhouse did a back flip and went cart wheeling and skipping out into the empty desert. It was an amusing lesson to us (if not to the outhouse occupant) to always make sure the area was clear behind the aircraft before running a power check on the engines.

Chapter 7—Combat Training

After we had accumulated approximately ten hours flying time we were divided into three groups and sent to what was called a P-38 operational training unit. Dick and I were among those transferred to a unit at Orange County Airport near Santa Ana, California. Others went to similar units at Santa Rosa, California, and Santa Maria, California.

Our training unit had some instructors who had completed combat in P-38s in the Pacific Theatre. We listened intently to their experiences and advice on tactics, as we had little idea of what to expect when we were in that position. The war was at about the half-way mark for the United States, with gains and reverses on both sides, so we knew there would be plenty for us to do no matter where we were sent.

The operations officer, Captain James Howard, had completed a tour overseas with General Chennault's Flying Tigers, so we felt fortunate to have that kind of experience to show us the ropes. Jimmie Howard was a quiet, lone-eagle type who often flew by himself. Whenever he was up, we knew there was a good possibility we'd be "bounced" by him. He'd always be up sun and would usually surprise us with a quick pass and be gone. He later went to England where he flew P-51s. He won the Medal of Honor by shooting down over five German Me 109 fighters during one mission. He was an outstanding pilot in the U.S. Army Air Corps.

We flew a lot of formation during which we often got into wild simulated dogfights with other P-38s or with any other type fighter that ventured into the area. The objective was to get on the tail of the opposing aircraft. This involved a lot of air maneuvering and sharp turns. Once on the tail of the "enemy" aircraft, that was considered sufficient to break off the engagement as a win. It would begin with four ships in a flight but often ended with complete breakup of the formation. As we were to learn, maintaining four-ship integrity while in a dog fight was just not sustainable or practical.

Air-to-air and air-to-ground gunnery was also on the agenda. Air-to-air was usually conducted on a range west of San Clemente Island (about 30 miles off the coast of Los Angeles), or over the west mountains of Death Valley. Air-to-ground gunnery was conducted at ranges on the Mojave Desert. Air-to-air gunnery involved shooting at a sleeve-type target drawn a hundred yards or so behind a slower tow aircraft or occasionally another P-38 flying slower than cruise speed. We would set up a pattern, with a single P-38 breaking off from a flight above and behind the tow plane. The single plane would then make a curved approach to the sleeve target, fire all four 50-caliber machine guns when in range from a deflected angle, then break off in time to avoid hitting the tow aircraft. This maneuver was then followed by a return to the flight above and behind the towed target to await a turn for another firing pass. Hitting the target was not easy because the sleeve was not very large and precision flying to avoid slip of the aircraft during the firing phase was essential to success. Determination of who got hits was made when the target was dropped back at the base. Each aircraft had color-coded bullets that left a color on the sleeve if it were hit and identified who had made hits.

Air-to-ground gunnery, including dive bombing, involved firing at (or dive bombing) old tanks, trucks, and military vehicles positioned in restricted areas on the Mohave Desert. Entry and use of these facilities was controlled by crews with radios at the site. Small practice bombs with very light charges were used for dive bombing practice.

Both air-to-air and air-to-ground gunnery brought us closer to what we might expect in actual combat. We could hear and feel the rapid fire of the machine guns and, by breaking sharply away from a dive bomb run, observe where the bomb actually struck. Safety of flight under both conditions had to be stressed because it was too easy to become fixed on the target and not break off at the proper moment or to fail to avoid other aircraft involved in the same activity. Both aspects of this part of our training had a special impact on us, because we realized that our ability to do that would have much to do with our success in combat. After gunnery over west Death Valley, we often flew down into the center of the valley for some practice at low-level flying, and also to note an unusual reading on the altimeter of a couple hundred feet below sea level.

We worked hard and learned a lot from our instructors. Best of all we were beginning to feel very much at home in the P-38. Each morning and evening there was a requirement to patrol the ocean off Los Angeles and along the coast looking for enemy subs. This gave us a small feeling of doing something constructive toward the war effort. We also got some night flying experience, which adds a whole new dimension to fighter operation.

The Los Angeles area was blanketed with anti-aircraft units which got their night training by tracking any aircraft flying over in the beam of powerful search lights, followed by simulated anti-aircraft batteries fire. Sometimes several searchlights would concentrate on one aircraft. If you looked down into them the intensity of the light would be blinding, so the procedure when that happened was to keep your head down, fly by instruments, and call the Los Angeles control center requesting them to cut off the searchlights

We had built up more than 85 hours of total P-38 time when we were alerted to get ready for transfer overseas. This meant sending your wife home if married, disposing of your car if you had one, getting all the necessary shots, and otherwise preparing to leave the country to participate in the war. We were briefed not to give dates of departure to anyone. Our orders were classified and only directed us to proceed by train to an overseas debarkation center at Miami.

I had gotten word home that overseas transfer was imminent, so a few days before we left, Mom made a trip to nearby Bellflower, California, where she stayed with friends and I was able to visit her for a few hours. I have often thought how difficult it must have been for her. She knew that I was headed for combat, but not where or for how long. I remember her well-intentioned words of advice: "Bob, please don't fly too high or too fast." She didn't know that too low and too slow was the worst thing to do. I reassured her as best I could, bid her a somber and somewhat emotional goodbye, and left feeling depressed over the possibility it might be the last time we ever saw each other. Back at the base a busy schedule of getting packed up and ready to travel to an unknown destination required my immediate attention, and the depression of leaving family and loved ones had to be sidelined.

About 65 of the original 80 volunteers had successfully completed the training program and gathered at the Los Angeles train station on May 15, 1943. We were put on our own special train of about five cars. The cars had been taken out of storage somewhere and were of an ancient variety with velvet-covered seats and stained-glass above the seat windows. The seats were hard and most of the windows were permanently stuck shut. One car had bunks so, except for a few hours leave in New Orleans, we lived, slept, and ate on the train. We took the southern route all the way, and it was hot through Arizona, Texas, and the southern states. Fortunately we did manage to pry open a few windows.

For reasons never explained (possibly to provide our own security in case of attempted sabotage), each of us had been issued a .45-caliber pistol with ammunition. A favorite pastime along the remote New Mexico and Texas route was to shoot at remote posts or various railroad lights, a practice probably not much appreciated by the railroad. Fortunately we were not very effective, and we all agreed we could more easily hit something from a moving train by throwing the .45 pistol at a target rather than firing at it.

It was a week-long trip, and the monotony of the train was difficult. At one stop in a small town in Texas near the Mexican border, one of the pilots volunteered to run over to a store we could see at a distance and bring back some much-needed cold drinks. We watched him come out of the store, arms loaded with frosty-looking, thirst-quenching soda pop, just as the train lurched forward to continue on its journey. Our benefactor quickened his pace to a fast walk, then a trot, then finally to a dead run as the train started to outdistance him. To gain speed he was forced to jettison a few bottles of the thirst-quenching liquid every few steps, finally having to drop the last of his load in order to make a flying leap for the last car. We felt like someone who had crawled across the desert only to find the oasis dry!

The trip seemed to go on forever, but on our arrival in New Orleans we were permitted to go to a hotel where we got a bath, a good meal, and a few hours to roam around the city. Finally the train trundled into Miami in May, 1943, and having survived the memorable if not comfortable train trip from Las Angeles, California, we began processing at the Miami overseas replacement center.

Chapter 8—North Africa and Hat in the Ring Squadron

Processing to go overseas consisted of getting any missing vaccinations, updating our personnel files, and receiving further travel orders. We still did not know officially where we were to be sent, but the general consensus was that it would be North Africa. Our travel orders directed us to an APO, a postal destination unknown to us. We were manifested on cargo-carrying C-46s, usually in groups of four or five per aircraft. The C-46s were filled with cargo so we found space wherever it was available. My transport carried a load of tires and tubes, with some of the tubes inflated, so they made a fairly comfortable bed. We headed down through South America and after several refueling stops arrived at Belem, Brazil, the jumping-off place for crossing the Atlantic to Africa via Ascension Island. This gave us a positive clue as to our destination—it had to be North Africa. We knew that there were three P-38 groups stationed in the Tunisia area and strongly suspected one or all of them could be our destination. We knew little more about the P-38 units or what their primary mission was other than air combat. We were to learn as time and our location dictated.

The trip to Belem was mostly over jungles and followed the Amazon River part of the way. Since almost all of us had never been out of the United States, it was quite a traveling experience. At Belem we stayed overnight and were fed pretty well. The mess hall was staffed with Brazilians whose English was limited. After our huge meal of meat, potatoes, and vegetables, one of the waiters kept coming over to me and saying what sounded like "meish meish?"

Thinking it must mean Brazilian for, "are you finished?" I nodded yes. He then took my plate away and brought it back loaded again with another helping of everything. The Portuguese "mais," it turned out, meant "more." We had a few hours to explore Belem, and it became apparent that the thing to buy was a kind of Chukka boot. They were

brown leather, slightly above ankle high, pull-on type boots. They were
built to last and were comfortable as well as somewhat distinctive, if not
regulation, to wear with an Army uniform. They only cost about $5 per
pair, so each of us bought a pair or two. They served us all throughout
the tour.

The next leg of the trip was to Ascension Island by C-54 air transport.
The flight was long but quite comfortable compared to riding on cargo
C-46s. Our stop at Ascension was only long enough for refueling and
a meal, and then we continued on. After another long flight we arrived
in Casablanca, French Morocco. This gave us some sense of location.
Arrival in Casablanca was met with great anticipation as most of us had
seen the iconic movie Casablanca. We were eager to find "Rick's Place!"

It was early June 1943, and Rommel's German Army was just being
pushed off the Bon Peninsula in Northern Tunisia after bitter and costly
air and land battles. Casablanca was a rear supply area and bustling with
activity. We were assigned a bunk in a large, transient officers' building
called the Hotel De Gink. It was an open-bay, barracks-type building
filled with Army cots, and we welcomed the chance to get some sleep. It
had been a long and wearing trip to a place that seemed light years away
from California.

We were now in another world, filled with Arabs and some "free
French" as they were called. There was a sense of urgency in the air as
the Army worked feverishly to set up a support complex. The city, not
only jammed with people, camels, and pull carts, now had military jeeps,
trucks, tanks, and all the other military equipment added. The result was
constant bedlam and confusion. The Moroccan French, who had had
some difficulty deciding which side to be on when the invasion of Africa
by Allied troops began near Casablanca, were obviously in control of
what little was left of the French Moroccan economy.

We were a bit awed by it all during the week. We awaited further
orders and had lots of time to visit the city. There was a bar named
"Rick's Place" after the movie Casablanca, so we got acquainted with

that. About the only drinks available were triple sec, a liqueur, and another they called peanut beer. Peanut beer was a washed-out kind of swill, only slightly resembling real beer and served barely cool. It gave us something to do as we began to pick up a few words of French and became acclimated to a strange land and strange people.

Finally orders directed us to an airfield about fifteen miles from Casablanca near a small village called Berchid. The Air Corps had hastily set up a combat training base for us and had assigned some P-38 pilots who had finished their combat tour to be our instructors. We now began living as we would for the rest of our tour, in tents and eating out of mess kits. The place was dusty and drab, helping us acclimate to what we would experience in the way of living conditions for the next year.

The P-38s assigned for the training were war weary and out of commission most of the time, while the instructor pilots understandably were war weary and anxious to return stateside. The final battles in North Africa had taken a heavy toll of fighter pilots, particularly during the battle for Kasserine Pass. Most of the missions had been dive bombing and strafing, a particularly vulnerable type of combat for a fighter because you must operate in range of every gun the enemy has on the ground. The well-intentioned program to give us a bit more combat training under experienced combat pilots never really got off the ground. In two or three weeks there my flying time amounted to about ten hours.

On one simulated (no actual firing) air-to-air gunnery mission my aircraft's radio was continuously emitting very loud static. On landing Dick Lee came up to say something to me and although I could see his lips moving there was no sound. It alarmed me to discover I was almost totally deaf. The flight surgeon looked me over, determined my eardrums were badly bruised, and grounded me for three days. By that time my hearing returned and became normal shortly thereafter.

During our stay at Berchid we roamed back into Casablanca a few more times. Since we were transient officers we found ourselves to be pretty much ostracized from the permanent party military around

Casablanca. We were barred from all of the support unit clubs and got quite a bit of harassment for not saluting every 1st lieutenant and above we passed on the street. They just couldn't bring themselves to accept those "unmilitary" looking officers, wearing leather jackets and crushed hats, the distinguishing mark of a fighter pilot. The unauthorized Brazilian boots also did not further enhance our military appearance.

Considering the quality of food and living conditions at Berchid, we strongly suspected that anything other than C-rations and Spam® was being siphoned off by the support personnel who lived in requisitioned hotels in Casablanca, although we never found out because we were never allowed in their clubs or mess halls. In a short time those members of the Atlantic Base Section had made themselves just about as popular with us as the enemy. For kicks we would sit at a sidewalk bar and sing, "Mother, take down your service flag, your son's in the ABS." This was not a positive contribution toward good relations with members of that organization, and we were all but barred from the city.

Finally word came that we were being assigned to combat units. This would undoubtedly be to one of the three groups (three squadrons each) of P-38s in three different locations in North Africa. We were split up and shipped out as replacement pilots to all three of them. Dick Lee and I along with twenty-five others of our volunteer group were assigned to the First Fighter Group, then stationed at a field called Mateur Air Base in Tunisia. The base was on a dry lake about fifteen miles east of the port of Bizerte. We were then further assigned to squadrons, and as luck would have it Dick Lee and I were both assigned to the 94th Fighter Squadron. We were ecstatic. The 94th had a wealth of history. It was leading ace Eddie Rickenbacker's squadron in World War I and remains active and famous as the "Hat in the Ring" squadron still. We felt that we couldn't have been better assigned if we had been allowed to choose any outfit in the Air Corps. Our only disappointment was that we had missed Eddie Rickenbacker himself, who had visited the squadron a couple of weeks earlier and had passed out Hat in the Ring pins to all the pilots

The author's Hat-in-the-Ring Squadron insignia, originated by leading ace Capt. Rickenbacker during World War I.

The 1st Fighter group had been in Africa since the Allied invasion the year before and had been through a lot. We felt pretty green alongside the older veteran combat pilots, but they were most happy to see replacements and to get the squadron back to full pilot strength again.

Living conditions at Mateur left much to be desired. We lived in four-man tents on the dry, cracked lakebed and slept on folding cots. Each of us had a metal mess kit and cup that we washed after eating. Washing the kit meant scrubbing everything in a barrel of hot GI soap and water, then rinsing in another barrel. By the end of the line the water turned to the consistency of soup and it became impossible to get all the grease and soap off. As a result there was a continuous round of diarrhea. We slept under mosquito netting and tucked it in pretty well because the dry cracked bed of the lake housed innumerable beetles and scorpions. It could be a painful mistake to put a boot on in the morning without first shaking it out good to make sure it wasn't already inhabited. Fortunately those in our tent escaped such an attack. A few makeshift showers had been rigged out of 50-gallon steel barrels, the water heated by the desert sun.

About the second day after arrival we were lined up with our mess kits for the evening meal when someone yelled, "Hey, Smoky!" I looked up to see an old high school classmate, Jack Held, ahead of me in line. He had been with the Group since it had been in England, and served as an armorer. We saw each other often after that, and he would always be at the flight line to meet me when I returned from a mission. Thanks to Jack, my high school nickname "Smoky" became my name to all the pilots from then on.

Summer had arrived and it was hot and dry with more than a little dust blowing about, although we did get used to it. The complete lack of color in an overseas combat outfit was at first a bit depressing. Everything, including our clothing, was light tan or olive drab. Our aircraft were camouflage painted, of course, and any support equipment including vehicles and anti-aircraft weapons were likewise painted or under camouflage netting.

The first few days were spent getting settled in and drawing our combat flight gear. Besides flight clothing, flying helmet, and stateside .45-caliber pistol, we were issued a parachute, switchblade knife, "Mae West" life jacket, oxygen mask, dinghy, canteen, and a survival kit. The knife was primarily for the purpose of stabbing the dinghy to deflate it in the event it accidentally inflated in the cockpit. The survival kit, along with the dinghy, was attached to the parachute pack and contained a machete, some hard chocolate, fishing line, pocket compass, and other necessities. The dinghy made up the seat of the parachute and had cans of fresh water and flares wrapped up in it. They were very necessary items, but when you sat on them for hours they let you know they were there right through the protective cushion as they imprinted on your backsides.

The 94th Fighter Squadron "Fearsome Foursome" classmates: Glenn Terry, Ralph Thiesen, Robert "Smoky" Vrilakas, and Dick Lee sporting newly-issued equipment at Mateur Air Base, Tunisia, 1943.

For those first few days the new pilots didn't fly, but we intently watched the squadrons take off and form up for missions and return. At that time they were in the process of softening up the island of Pantelleria, just off the coast of Tunisia. The island was still being stubbornly held by German and Italian troops.

Author with an abandoned German Me 109
at Mateur Air Base, Tunisia, September 1943.

We had been assigned to tent quarters with a couple of the older pilots, who we listened to with great awe and respect. There were a lot of combat stories and some good friendly advice, most of which was to "stay in formation; don't straggle because the enemy fighters will jump a straggler first." Plus, "keep your eyes open and your head on a swivel because the enemy always comes out of the sun and will be on you before you know it." We were emphatically told that our primary purpose on a bomber escort mission was to protect the bombers, and not be lured off to attack a distant fighter because that was often a decoy by the enemy to get you away from the bombers. We learned that our air operations included most of the German-occupied countries in the Mediterranean area. This was extended later to include the southern edge of Germany. Also, the Luftwaffe pilots had the benefit of a lot of experience as well as the advantage of fighting over their own territory. If they were shot down or crash landed and survived they could return to fly again. If we, on the other hand, were downed over enemy territory and survived, we would most likely end up in a German prison camp. We wondered what it would feel like to be on a real combat mission. We were to find out soon enough.

Dick Lee and I were soon scheduled for a local flight with the squadron commander, Major Wellensiek. He told us beforehand we would just fly formation, but warned us he might be pretty erratic and to be ready for quick turns. He obviously wanted to be sure we could stay in formation and handle the airplane. The flight went well with Dick and I glued to his wing all the way. We liked the landing pattern, which involved flying low down the active runway at about 300 mph in echelon (all pilots in a flight staggered wing tip to wing tip on one side or the other of the flight leader, depending on the direction of the intended landing pattern). After flying low the length of the landing runway, the leader would peel up and around the landing pattern in a tight turn. The rest of the flight would peel off individually at about four second intervals, space themselves in the pattern at the proper interval, and follow each other in for landing. When this procedure was properly executed, it made for a tight pattern in a kind of oblong circle that got several flights down in minimum time. A good pattern required the flight leader to stay in a bank all the way around, rolling out just in time to flare for landing. A victory roll was allowed in the pattern if a victory had been obtained and the pilot felt like it.

On landing Major Wellensiek said "Okay, we'll be scheduling you for a mission in the next day or two." He did not say more, but lack of any criticism left us feeling that we had proved our ability to fly formation and handle the aircraft. I now had a total of about 95 P-38 hours and a grand total of just over 300 flying hours. My training was finished except for upcoming on-the-job training and experience.

P-38s on approach for landing after a mission. The leader has just started his peel up for landing. Foggia, Italy, 1943.

Chapter 9—First Combat Mission

D Day for the invasion of Sicily was July 10, 1943, and the 1st Fighter Group was detached to North African Tactical Air Forces, which meant a rapid scale of operation not experienced before. The pilots, with me now among them, were expected to make as many as four missions per day if necessary. My first mission was on July 15, 1943, a day or two after the flight with the squadron commander. Scheduled pilots were notified the night before and given the time for mission briefing the next day, usually early in the morning. Either the squadron intelligence officer or the flight surgeon would awaken you in time for breakfast. I don't think I slept well that night, and breakfast of powdered eggs was particularly unappetizing.

Pilots from all the squadrons scheduled on the mission gathered at the Group briefing tent the next morning. The mission operations briefing consisted of the designated target, en route time, routes, altitudes, alternate target, anticipated enemy ground and air opposition plus expected weather en route, over target, and back at home base. Other information included meeting time and rendezvous point with bombers when applicable, radio frequencies, call signs, form-up procedures, and armament to be carried. Intelligence briefed us on known enemy aircraft and anti-aircraft en route and in the target area plus escape and evasion routes or tactics if we should go down over enemy territory. On occasion a special briefing by the Group commander would follow. A more detailed description of a specific mission will follow later on my 19th mission.

The first thing that everyone looked at upon entering the briefing tent was a large aerial map of Southern Europe and the Mediterranean Sea. A string running from home base to the target gave an immediate indication of where and how rough the mission might be. When the string ran up to Munich or to the Ploesti Oil Fields, which happened later on, there would be audible groans from the pilots. The briefings were

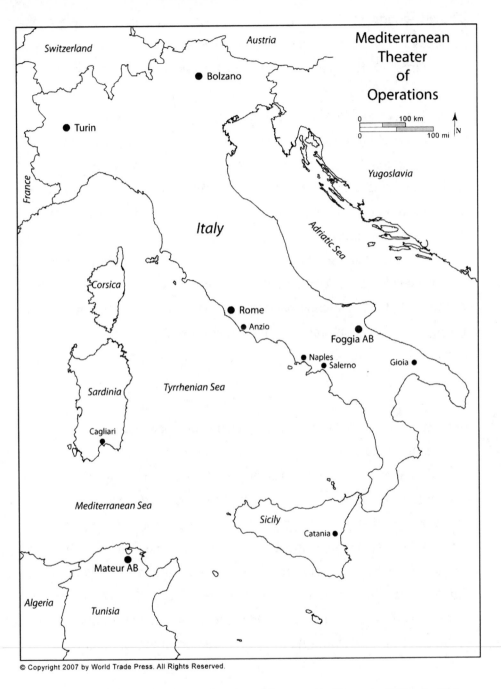

Map of Mediterranean area showing Mateur Air Base and North Africa.
(Map printed with permission from World Trade Press--
©Copyright 2007 by World Trade Press. All rights reserved.)

generally conducted by the Group operations officer, intelligence officer, and weather forecaster with occasional special briefings if necessary.

The mission that day, in support of American Army ground troops, was to dive bomb a German motor park. The target was near Randazzo, Sicily. The scheduled pilots gathered in the group mission briefing tent about an hour before takeoff. They sat on rough benches dressed in their flight suits. Some smoked cigarettes and there were always a few tension-relieving jokes. Because of possible compromise of classified information we couldn't write much on paper, so we often wrote essential information like start times, takeoff, and target times on the back of our hands since that could easily be smudged or rubbed off if necessary. Finally we were given a time hack to synchronize our watches and issued escape packets. The escape packets were sealed and carried in a flight suit pocket. They contained foreign money for the countries we would traverse plus a small United States flag and a map of the area. Not to be left out, the group chaplain would ask a blessing, and then we would be on our way to the flight line, usually by jeep. The trip also took us by personal equipment storage to pick up our parachutes and oxygen equipment on the way to our respective aircraft.

It was a general rule that a new pilot flew his first few missions as wingman to the assigned squadron flight commander for that mission. That was the most protected position and the easiest to fly. From there he would be assigned to element wingman, "Tail-End Charlie." This was the most vulnerable position because you were the farthest back in the flight of four. The squadron operations officer, Captain Hagenback, who flew as squadron leader that day, told me just to fly good formation on his aircraft and do everything he did to include dropping my bombs when he dropped his. We had to maintain strict radio silence even for takeoff so as not to compromise the mission. Generally there would be little or no radio transmissions between aircraft until we sighted enemy aircraft or had reached the target area. On the return from the target it was a different story. The enemy knew we were there and had us on their radar so there wasn't anything to compromise by using the radio.

Each aircraft had an assigned crew chief, and each pilot was assigned his own aircraft and crew chief. My crew chief was a young staff sergeant from Ohio named Chet Bala.

Author's crew chief,
Staff Sergeant Chet Bala,
whose conscientious maintenance
kept the P-38s flying, 1943.

He was very conscientious and serious about his job, and I had immediate respect for him and confidence in his ability to maintain a P-38.

The quality of aircraft maintenance meant life or death and we knew the crew chiefs worked under extremely difficult conditions, often having to scrounge parts or work long hours to get the aircraft ready on time for a mission. Chet Bala was a modest individual who took a lot of pride in maintaining his airplane and was always totally honest and forthright in keeping me posted on anything about the plane that wasn't up to snuff.

I regretted losing track of him after the war, but miraculously, through the Internet, was able to contact his descendents recently. He had married and fathered four children but, sadly, had died of a sudden heart attack at middle age.

An armorer also attended the plane and would install whatever armament was scheduled for the mission plus load the four .50-caliber machine guns and 20-mm cannon. They would paste a patch over the end of each gun barrel. This served to keep dirt, rain, or ice out of the barrel prior to use. It was also the first thing the crew chief looked at on your return to tell whether or not you had experienced combat on that mission. I probably enjoyed a bit of extra attention from the armorers because my friend Jack Held always gave my aircraft a second check.

Two 500-pound bombs (one under each wing) were set up for my first mission. I had never dropped a live, real bomb before. When attached they added an element of risk in that they could inadvertently be dropped during taxi or takeoff. They were designed so that they would not be armed until dropped a certain distance, however. Still, I was a bit shocked the first time I saw an armament crew kick a couple of them off the back of their truck. But that was done routinely without serious incident even though not a recommended practice.

After preflight inspection of the aircraft it was time to get set in the cockpit and be ready to start engines exactly on the time briefed. Chet Bala always climbed up on the wing and helped me get settled. The Mae West life jacket, unlike later styles, was bulky and made of stiff, rubberized canvas that managed to rub your neck raw before the completion of a mission. Between it, the parachute with dinghy and survival kit attached, the .45 pistol and water canteen, it was awkward getting into the cockpit and strapped down. Something was always catching on part of the aircraft. There was always a feeling of mounting nervous tension too, at that point, and it seemed easy to fumble at every latch or snap that had to be attended to. It's particularly worse on your first mission, but is always there. Fortunately, once off the ground things improve immensely.

Chet crouched on the wing and talked to me about the airplane, and I could tell he knew it intimately. It helped to fill the time of growing tension, and he stayed there until both engines were started and running smoothly. He did that on every mission and at the last moment would slide off the wing, latch the entrance ladder, and go out front waiting for my signal to be marshaled out of the revetment to the taxiway. He would always be there to meet me on my return, "sweating me out" as it was called.

The squadron leader started taxiing out so I moved out to follow him to the end of the runway. At the end of the runway we both went through our individual pre-takeoff engine checks and procedures, then on a green light from the tower lined up on the runway in much the same position as we would be in flight. The runway was too narrow to permit takeoff together, so as soon as he applied power I did also, holding the aircraft with the brakes until he started to rotate for lift off. Once in the air he would start a slow turn while I followed in a sharper turn inside to catch up. The turn would be continued until the rest of his flight joined up and eventually the other two flights. Once the squadron formed he would then continue in a turn to join up with the lead squadron or to allow the other squadrons to join up as required. This mission required only one squadron, the 94th.

The squadron in flight normally consisted of three flights of four aircraft each. A flight consisted of the flight leader and wingman and an element leader and wingman all in close formation (three- or four-foot wing side clearance and about a ten-foot interval). Each squadron had a call sign (the 94th at the time was Springcap, the 27th was Petdog, and the 71st was Cragmore) and each flight in squadron was designated as Red, White, or Blue flight. The call sign of any member of the squadron was determined by his flight color designation and assigned position. For example Red 1 would be the leader, Red 2 his wingman, Red 3 the element leader, and Red 4 the element leader's wingman.

I closed in tightly on Red 1 and, immediately after the squadron form up was completed, we turned north climbing en route to about 8,000 feet. We passed over Tunis and then continued out to sea over the Mediterranean. The island of Pantelleria appeared, but I was too busy keeping tight formation to watch the scenery. After about an hour and a half flight time there was a glimpse of land in the distance, and for the first time I saw enemy territory. Radio silence prevailed as the squadron leader began a descent toward the shore and the target. His job was much more complicated as he had to navigate very accurately and position the squadron so that we could dive bomb without having made our position known to the enemy any sooner than necessary. At the last moment he broke radio silence, telling us to arm our bombs (an arming wire controlled from the cockpit readied the bomb for release) and echelon to the right. An echelon formation made it possible to follow the leader into the target on pretty much the same flight path.

There was obviously a heavy battle in progress on the ground as we could see numerous fires and smoke and haze in the target area was thick. I heard my flight leader announce the start of his run and followed slightly in trail as we heeled over and started a steep dive. At his command to "drop bombs—now" I pressed the bomb release button. They were on the way and I had fired my first shot. The radio was then filled with indistinguishable chatter between aircraft as we started our climb back up, reformed, and headed back home. A few black puffs of flak appeared, but surprise had been on our side so that we were in and out before the ground fire could get very organized. The German 88mm cannon was an excellent weapon. Unlike our 90mm at the time, the 88mm could fire horizontally at ground targets and/or vertically at aircraft. When concentrated for air defense it could be devastating, particularly to bombers since they couldn't maneuver enough to provide effective countermeasures. Fighters could lessen the threat considerably by frequently changing course and altitude.

We proceeded directly back to base, relaxing by flying a loose formation and then tightening up on approach to the base for landing. It was a morale boost to the ground troops and a matter of pride to the pilots to look as sharp as possible at that point. We always approached the runway echeloned to the right or left as appropriate and at an altitude of about 100 feet over the runway, then did a "peel up" and landing pattern as previously described. Chet Bala was there to marshal me into the respective parking spot and was on the wing as soon as the engines were shut down, helping me get unstrapped and out of the cockpit. The mission had lasted three hours.

We were picked up in jeeps and taken directly to the group debriefing tent where the group and squadron intelligence officers wanted to know everything about the mission. It wasn't until then I learned two of our squadron pilots in another flight had collided over the target and gone straight in with their bombs. I had not, as yet, become acquainted with either of the pilots involved in the tragic event, but it drove home a valuable lesson—not to become so fixed on a target that you are not fully aware of the other aircraft involved from your unit, an experience that was forcibly demonstrated on a strafing sortie several missions later. I was a bit chagrined that it had escaped my notice, but the squadron commander assured me I had done exactly as he had wanted me to do—stay right in formation and concentrate only on that. I told myself from thereon I was going to take in more of the big picture. The loss of a pilot on any mission was a difficult matter to accept and emphatically brought home the tragic and sad consequences of war.

Chapter 10—Missions Two to Four: First Dogfight and a Fuel Management Mistake

My second mission on July 20 was a fighter sweep off the coast of Italy, and the type pilots liked to fly. It meant that rather than be on the defensive protecting bombers we could be looking for the enemy on our own terms, maybe even having the advantage of surprise and altitude for a change. This time I was assigned as Blue 2. Major Otto Wellensiek led the squadron that day and we were only one squadron in strength for the mission. After takeoff and form up we headed out across the Mediterranean at about 500 feet to avoid enemy radar detection, flying past Sicily toward the Bay of Naples. The white shoreline of the Sicilian coast appeared dimly in the distance while the Mediterranean Sea below became a darker blue. An occasional fishing boat bobbed on the water near the shore, but on this day I was more intensely focused on flying good formation.

We stayed off the coast of Italy looking for anything flying. It wasn't long until someone called in a "bogie" low and straight ahead of us. Sure enough there was a two-engine Italian SM.82 transport plane lumbering along below. It was considered "meat on the table," but our flight met with disappointment when we were ordered to climb to 3,000 feet and provide top cover. We watched enviously as Red flight pulled up behind the transport and started firing. I saw the tracers and puffs of smoke from the guns of the P-38s as they fired. Miraculously the SM.82 continued on its course as if oblivious to it all. After a couple of more passes by Red flight (while the rest of us yearned for a piece of the action) the SM.82 started a descent toward the water, finally flaring out and belly landing in the Mediterranean. Either they had been hit or got a strong message.

That sea landing counted as a "destroyed," so we proceeded on up the coast for another 15 or 20 minutes looking for more but with no success. On the way back some time later we were surprised to see the transport still afloat in the water with three or four Italians standing on the wings. We buzzed them and they waved as we went over, no doubt immensely relieved they hadn't been strafed. We never knew whether or not they were rescued, but they had a good chance since they weren't far offshore.

The mission took four hours ten minutes. With more than seven hours of combat time, I began to feel less like a raw recruit, but that was only the beginning.

Except for certain special occasions, mission scheduling provided each pilot a break of two to four days between missions, although the squadron fielded one mission or more almost every day. Bad weather at the base or the target could cause the whole squadron or group to stand down, but during the summer, weather was not a factor. Between missions, our time was pretty much our own. We played volleyball, wrote letters home, played cards, or just had flying talk sessions with each other. Occasionally we would be required to test hop a P-38 locally to confirm satisfactory maintenance or "slow fly" an airplane to break in a new replacement engine. As commissioned officers we also had the job of censoring outgoing personal mail of the enlisted men. It was a tedious and boring job and one we didn't particularly like, since we felt we were put in the undesirable position of snooping into their personal life. Despite continual cautions from security officials, some of the letters would divulge our location or strengths and losses. When that occurred the scissors were applied leaving gaping holes in the middle of a piece of correspondence. It was necessary but had to have been disconcerting to the recipient of such a letter.

The coastal town of Bizerte was about fifteen miles west of us, so on occasion when a jeep, command car, or truck could be spared we'd go in for Post Exchange supplies and a look around. Bizerte was a very active port for military logistics and was covered with barrage balloons. It was bombed occasionally at night by German bombers. Each tent at our base had a foxhole for such an event so when an air raid warning

sounded we sat beside our respective diggings in a total blackout while
the bombers passed directly overhead on their bomb run. It was an eerie
feeling to have the enemy bombers passing so low overhead we could
hear them clearly and occasionally pick out a dim shadow of them in
the darkness of night. They blasted the port quite heavily a few times
and we could hear the bomb strikes and observed some large resulting
fires. The British put up some night fighters and a lot of ground fire with
some success. The Germans apparently were aware of the anti-aircraft
barrage balloons and kept their altitude above them. On one such attack
we learned that a ship carrying a number of nurses (there was an army
hospital in Bizerte) was hit in the harbor and there had been numerous
casualties among them. The enemy was aware of an impending invasion
of the Italian mainland by the Allied forces and hoped to forestall it by
hitting at any gathering of ships in the harbor.

My third mission, on July 23, 1943, was to escort a rescue PBY
(a pontoon-equipped aircraft) to the Bay of Naples. There were some
downed crew members believed to be in the vicinity of the Isle of Capri.
Although we entered an area heavily defended by enemy fighters and
anti aircraft guns, we didn't encounter either. No downed airmen were
located so it was concluded they had been picked up by the Germans or
Italians, a very likely possibility considering the proximity to shore. The
mission turned out to be a "milk run" but it provided good training for
those of us who were somewhat new to the game.

My fourth mission, on August 1, 1943, was also an air-sea rescue
on which we escorted a PBY to the southern coast of Sardinia. I had
now permanently left the wing of the squadron leader and graduated to
the number 2 position in White Flight. The 94th was the only squadron
assigned to the mission. The PBY, a two-engine, pontoon-equipped
rescue aircraft, was very slow so we had to do a lot of weaving over it
to keep it ahead of us. We approached to about a mile off the coast of
Sardinia where the PBY spotted two airmen in dinghies on the water. The
PBY dropped smoke flares to get wind direction and mark their position,

then set up a pattern and landed near them. As they taxied toward the dinghies, several shore batteries opened up and spouts of water erupted near the PBY and downed flyers.

About the same time someone called out enemy fighters (bogies) above us and toward the sun. The squadron leader ordered us to drop our belly tanks to provide needed maneuverability and lessen the fire hazard. After pressing the release button for the belly tanks there was an immediate improved difference in aircraft handling. Within seconds however, both of my engines quit, and I started dropping out of formation. My first thought was that I'd been hit by the enemy fighters, but then the realization came that in the excitement of seeing enemy fighters for the first time, a very important procedure had been overlooked—I hadn't switched the fuel selectors to main aircraft fuel tanks before dropping the belly tanks! Not having done that the fuel source to both engines had been cut off. After quickly selecting main tanks and switching on the fuel boost pumps, the engines restarted immediately, and as I headed back into the formation the flight leader called, "White 2, what's wrong?"

By this time the German fighters, Me 109s, had started their passes at us. Generally they would Split S from one to two thousand feet above and onto the last aircraft of one of the flights. A Split S maneuver, if you are not familiar with the term, was to turn the aircraft on its back, then pull it into a vertical dive to within target range. This was the fastest way to put a fighter in a dive and to avoid negative gravity pull, or weightlessness. The maneuver was also the quickest way to put the attacking aircraft in position to get effective fire. After making a firing pass, the maneuver ended with a pull up back to altitude or, if exposed to one of our fighters, another Split S down and out of the area. This gave them plenty of speed and if not challenged they would continue the attack from the rear firing until the last second, then pull straight back up to get set for another pass. Normally if our flights were all intact we "broke," that is, made a sharp turn into the attacking aircraft, on the command of the squadron leader (e.g. "flights break left—now"). In a heavy battle where the squadron and flights might get broken up or when simultaneous enemy attacks were made, we would break on our own depending on a particular circumstance. Generally, once one or more of our aircraft faced the German fighter, he would roll over and Split S into a dive down and away from us. They had the greatest respect for the four .50-caliber machine guns and 20-mm cannon mounted in the nose of a P-38. It was tempting to follow but that could mean leaving the bombers, or whoever you were escorting, vulnerable to other enemy fighters. On this mission there were only three of the enemy and their purpose seemed mostly to harass us in the hope they might pick off a straggler. Had my fuel situation not been straightened out quickly they may not have been disappointed.

After several passes at us, during which we kept turning into them, they turned and headed back inland, probably getting low on fuel. Our flight did not get a shot at them, and if there were any taken by the other flights they were not effective. About the time our fracas broke up the PBY called to say they had the two men who had been in the water aboard, and were now airborne and heading back to base. We then picked up the PBY and escorted it out of danger. I kept thinking how those two airmen must have felt having been picked out of the water just off the enemy's shore. I could picture myself in their position and imagine how relieved and grateful they must have been to see friendly aircraft above them and to be snatched from under the noses of the enemy. Had they been taken prisoner they would have spent endless days in an enemy prisoner of war camp. The stature of air-sea rescue has always remained high with me. In all conflicts they have made some remarkable rescues under extremely dangerous conditions, often with little fanfare or recognition for some very heroic efforts.

As we approached the coast of Africa there was a sudden loss of oil from my left engine. It was only a matter of seconds before the oil pressure would go completely, so rather than run the risk of ruining an engine and possible fire, I shut it down. It was the first actual loss of an engine I'd experienced. The landing went fine and served as a great confidence builder concerning the capability of the aircraft to fly on single engine. An oil line had broken loose and oil was rapidly pumped from the engine.

At debriefing I had to (with a certain amount of embarrassment) explain the sudden fall out of formation. The rest of the pilots recognized it as a rookie error or similar to an experience they may have had and accepted my explanation without question. It was a valuable lesson to me, the consequences of which did not go unnoticed, so that mistake was never repeated.

Chapter 11—Missions Five to Fifteen

At about this time word was passed down from group headquarters that maintenance was having a difficult time due to low manning. All the pilots were directed to go down to the flight line during non-flight days and help their crew chief in any way possible. Sgt. Bala looked at me somewhat dubiously when I "reported for duty" and after some thought (and probably no little concern for the welfare of the airplane) said, "Well, you could clean the landing gear oleo struts." Since they collapsed much like a shock absorber and were subject to a lot of flying dirt during takeoff and landings, it was necessary to clean them often. So with a bucket of solvent and rag I went to work. The crew chiefs no doubt got a kick out of putting all those officers to work, but that kind of teamwork was good for morale and to get the job done. We did that for a week or two then fell back into our old routine.

For my fifth mission, on August 5, I was in the Blue 2 position for my first B-17 bomber escort. It was to Catania, Sicily, to attack bridges near that city where the 8th Army was stalled. After takeoff and form up we joined the bombers near Tunis and flew about 1,000 feet above them. We had to continually crisscross since the B-17s were considerably slower. We could also get a better view of the sky above and around them by weaving back and forth over their formation. As the bombers reached the shore and started the bomb run we encountered very heavy flak. Flak was simply a bursting anti-aircraft artillery shell put up in a boxlike pattern, usually concentrated over the bomb run path. It would explode in a large puff of black smoke, and when concentrated the smoke from them seemed to cover the entire sky around the bombers. You could see the bursts tracking the bomber formation and the adjustments being made by the enemy gunners in altitude and azimuth or lead. Occasionally the bursts would be directed at us, at which time we'd abruptly change direction. The bombers couldn't do that when on their bomb run, so they were particularly vulnerable. Fortunately, we couldn't hear the bursts unless they were very close. If one survived an audible burst, it was very likely that a shell fragment had hit somewhere on the aircraft, and it might be one that would disable or knock your aircraft out of the sky. On a different mission one of the pilots in the group experienced a direct hit in the wing of his P-38 by an anti-aircraft projectile. It passed through the wing of his P-38, but fortunately did not explode—a very narrow escape from being obliterated. Had we not been spared the noise of all the anti-aircraft shells exploding, we'd probably have suffered the same shock effects that ground troops experienced during heavy artillery attacks.

No enemy fighters appeared during the bomb run so we could watch the bombs hitting the harbor below. The target area seemed to erupt with smoke, fire, and dust. It wouldn't be possible to assess the damage fully until later when reconnaissance photo aircraft took pictures.

As we turned back, though, about fifteen enemy Me 109 fighters appeared. In the ensuing action, during which we were able to prevent any fighter attack on the bombers, Lt. Herr from the 94th became the victim of a malfunctioning compass. Disoriented and running out of fuel, he bailed out off the coast of Sardinia. After three weeks in a dingy in the Mediterranean, he was finally picked up by a passing freighter and taken to North Africa. His weight when he returned to the squadron was down to 100 pounds. He was returned to the United States where he became a very convincing instructor in a survival school.

My sixth mission, as White 2, on August 6, was to Angitola, Italy, to strafe trains and installations. We flew low over the Mediterranean to avoid enemy radar. At Angitola we came in over the rail yard with complete surprise and strafed railroad cars, some of which exploded, indicating they were carrying ammunition. Surprise on such a mission was all-important because if the enemy were aware they could put up a wall of ground fire. The Germans had special cars on most of their military trains, which were heavily armed with anti-aircraft weapons. They looked like any other rail car but on attack the car siding could be dropped to permit some very concentrated and effective fire. A cardinal rule was that you made one pass only at a ground target then went on to the next. To pull up, go around, and attack the same target a second time was to invite disaster, because the element of surprise would be gone and the enemy would be waiting with everything they had.

My seventh mission, on August 7, was a B-26 bomber escort to Naples, Italy, and my first assignment as "Tail-End Charlie," the number four man in a flight and the most vulnerable position. My assigned position was White 4. The B-26s were low-altitude, twin-engine bombers. They were slow and usually went into the target area at 8,000 to 12,000 feet. They always seemed to just hang in the sky, particularly in the target area, and were very vulnerable to anti-aircraft fire and enemy fighters. The Germans and Italians were anticipating an invasion of the Italian mainland, so the Naples area was heavily fortified and we encountered considerable flak going in. As the bombers made their run, we were jumped by a fairly large number of German fighters and a very active air battle ensued. The B-26s made it in and out without a loss so we had done our job. My record does not show any claims for damaged or destroyed enemy aircraft although we all got some shots.

My eighth mission, on August 8, was a dive-bombing and strafing mission to East Italy around the Bova area. I did not record what we dive-bombed, but it was probably a railroad bridge. After dive bombing we followed the railroad tracks looking for trains and depots to strafe. My position was White 4. We approached a small railroad depot at Cape Spartivento, Italy, and strafed several cars on a siding plus the depot itself. Pieces flew off the boxcars and depot as my .50 calibers hit. Lt. Terry, one of my classmates, was flying Tail-End Charlie position in an adjoining flight. He went into a descending strafing run but never pulled out. We watched helplessly as his plane hit the tracks and exploded into a fireball. He had no chance to get out of it at that altitude, and we surmised later that he must have taken a direct hit in the cockpit and was killed or rendered unconscious before crashing. There was no indication of his trying to pull up. Lt. Terry, from Seaside, Oregon, was a very popular member of my cadet class and an excellent pilot. We felt particularly bad about his and Lt. Grieshaber's loss. Lt. Grieshaber met a similar fate on the same mission. He was hit, caught fire, and belly landed in the water off the Italian coast. He was one of the older, more experienced pilots in the squadron. I did not know him well, but learned later he had survived the belly landing in the sea, made it to shore, and was then captured by German troops. They shot and killed him, apparently without provocation, on the spot.

Ken Meyers, a relative of Lt. Grieshaber, visited Cape Spartivento in 2003 and took this photograph of the shoreline where Lt. Grieshaber was shot and killed by the Germans. The restored railroad depot the author strafed on his eighth mission in 1943 is visible in this photograph.

We concluded afterward that some of the rail cars on the siding had been anti-aircraft cars and that the enemy had been forewarned we were en route.

Loss of the two pilots was a bitter loss and shockingly brought the reality of war and combat to me. To lose a classmate and one that I had trained with for some time was particularly difficult to accept. He was an impressive individual, of flawless character, and an excellent pilot. His erect bearing, fair complexion, sunny smile, and pleasant personality had made him a popular figure among us. He typified an "all American" boy.

We felt despondent about the losses but could not dwell on them. Such a loss wasn't discussed much at the time. That didn't mean they were forgotten, it meant that we had to try to put our grief on the back burner until the war was over. In 1988 I had the honor of being the principal speaker and to meet Lt. Terry's two living sisters and relatives at a memorial for him at Tillamook, Oregon, his home town.

My ninth mission, on August 12, was an air-sea rescue mission off Sardinia. I flew Red 2 position. We were briefed that the mission would be a long one so we carried belly fuel tanks and a canteen of water. It was a very hot day and we flew at 300 to 500 feet off the water following a PBY in a search pattern. It was hot in the cockpit and my canteen of water was gone after about two hours. I should have rationed myself. After about five hours of flying some flares fired from the water revealed a dinghy with two men in it. By the time they had been picked up and we got back to base, we had flown seven and a half hours. Having sat that long in the cramped, strapped-down position, and after becoming thoroughly dehydrated, I couldn't move to get out of the cockpit after landing. Chet Bala helped undo my parachute straps and half pulled me out onto the wing. No doubt everything in my seat and backpack was thoroughly imprinted on my backsides and my flight suit was caked with perspiration salt.

My tenth mission was on Friday, August 13, and was the kind that brought audible groans from the pilots at the group briefing. The string on the map stretched all the way up to Rome, with the Littorio airfield and the San Lorenzo and Vittorio railroad marshaling yards the targets for the B-26 low-altitude bombers. At this point Sicily was in the bag, and it was obvious we were beginning the softening up process preliminary to an Allied invasion of the Italian mainland. My record doesn't show my flying position but it must have been at #4 Tail-End Charlie. Both the 1st Fighter Group and the 82nd Fighter Group participated in escorting one hundred B-26 bombers. We were briefed in detail about avoiding any damage to the Vatican and on escape and evasion procedures should we go down in that area. Intelligence indicated heavy anti-aircraft and enemy fighter concentration in the Rome area.

They were right on both counts. We first encountered very heavy flak. It suddenly halted over the target, and about 25 to 30 Me 109s and Machi 202s jumped us. A general melee followed during which I got several deflection shots at three or four fighters, although I couldn't verify any downed. We worked the bombers back out of the Rome area and finally got them safely out to sea. There were no fighter losses on our side, but a loss of two B-26s. The opposition up to this point had not been particularly intense, but that condition was short lived. The Germans, anticipating the Allied invasion of Italy, began markedly increasing their air strength. The mission lasted five and a half hours and left us pretty exhausted.

Over the next few weeks, I flew three more escort missions over Italy, encountering flak but no fighter opposition. It appeared that either we were beginning to gain control of the airspace over Italy, or the Luftwaffe was busy getting additional forces placed and ready for the expected Allied invasion. Later in August it became apparent the Luftwaffe force in Italy had been heavily augmented and strengthened in that area. Apparently realizing we were gaining the upper hand over Italy, on August 17 and 18, 1943, the Germans conducted night air raids on Bizerte. Their bomb run again took them directly over our airfield, so we got a first-hand view of it from beside our foxholes.

On August 22 I flew my 14th mission, escorting B-26s to Naples in the Blue 2 position, and this time there was plenty of action. We were jumped by approximately 40 Me 109s and a few Machi 202s, and both sides got lots of shots. I got several bursts off from a deflected angle, and although I was sure of some hits there wasn't time enough to review the results, so I wasn't able to make any claims. As soon as one fighter broke down and away there would be another to contend with. For the first time I saw some of the enemy fighters approaching the bombers flying upside down. If they got close enough to a bomber, the pilot would fire and then

Split S down and out of range of both the bomber gunners and the fighter escort. We kept the bombers protected with no losses, so accomplished the mission successfully. An enemy aircraft destroyed would have of course been icing on the cake. The mission took about four hours and forty-five minutes.

We noted a particular rash of aggressiveness by the enemy at this time, which was later believed to be the work of an elite Luftwaffe fighter Gruppe or Jagdgeschwader, which had recently arrived from the Russian front on its way to Western Europe to confront the growing threat of the Eighth Air Force in England and the Allied invasion of Italy. A large number of the enemy aircraft had yellow noses, possibly one of Goering's Group, and were flown with marked expertise. They came into our formation with an altitude advantage and dove steeply to attack. They seldom stayed to maneuver, but dove on downward, with the usual tactic of pulling up at a distance and back to an altitude advantage. It was by far the most sustained resistance yet encountered.

At this time for about a week the Group had us practicing formation at low altitude in the local area of Mateur Air Base and the Mediterranean coast. We'd fly to a predetermined point, make a practice strafing run over it, and return to base. The reason for this training was very secret and since we didn't need to know at that point we weren't told. We knew something different was coming, however.

One incident occurred during a practice session, which could have been a bit disastrous. At very low altitude we popped up over a hill near the coast and found ourselves heading right under the barrage balloons at Biserte Harbor. Someone called out "barrage balloons" and the whole formation broke up. Everyone went on his own, pulling up, down, or making an immediate 180-degree turn. The prospect of hitting a barrage balloon cable was imminent, but fortunately we all got out of the area without mishap. There were several close encounters between P-38s and the cables. At debriefing the leader was made fully aware he had badly goofed.

Mission 15 on August 24, 1943, cleared up the mystery of all the low altitude practice. Intelligence had determined that the Foggia area near the "spur" on the boot of Italy was the location of a large concentration of the German and Italian airfields and aircraft. It was decided at a higher level of command to commit all three P-38 fighter groups into one big strafing mission with the hope that we could deal a very serious blow to the enemy capability by knocking them out on the ground. The previous night British bombers had dropped time-delayed bombs on the airfield complex. It was theorized that would keep them pretty busy on the ground at the time we would conduct the mass strafing. The time delays on the bombs were varied up to several hours duration.

We were briefed to stay under 200-feet altitude for the entire 530 miles to target in order to avoid enemy radar and to enter around the "spur" of the boot of Italy. Once past the spur we were to line up abreast and make a straight-ahead strafing run through the Foggia Air Base complex. With the three combined groups involved there would be over 100 P-38s crossing the area at once. We were cautioned not to vary our course once approaching over the target area. The congestion of so many raised a high risk of colliding with one another.

We were also briefed on another important target. The Germans had somehow obtained a P-38, probably one that crash landed behind enemy lines. They had repaired it and were flying it in combat. During a B-17 bombing mission it approached a B-17 bomber formation and shot a B-17 down, so it posed a threat to any Allied aircraft over Italy. We were of course concerned it might join our formation on any mission, and, understandably, it made the gunners of the bombers very trigger-happy.

A standard procedure to use if we lost an engine over the target area and did not have escort from our own fighters was to feather up the dead engine and join up with the bombers by flying close formation with them. It was better than nothing since the turret gunners on the bombers could provide some protection. Because of the enemy P-38, the procedure was modified to the effect that instead of flying directly into the bomber formation, we would fly alongside well out of their gun range then slowly slide over to join up without ever pointing our nose at them. Failing to do that left a pretty good chance they would open up with all that they had. I had just such an experience on one mission when I had to feather an engine on the way out of the target area. As I carefully slipped my aircraft sideways toward the bombers, and after settling into formation with one of them, I looked over to see all the guns on about six or seven B-17s trained directly on me. It was a bit like facing a firing squad as I waved at the gunners in my most friendly fashion.

One group of P-38s appeared like a sizeable force in the air. Three times that many seemed to fill the sky as we rendezvoused off the coast of Tunisia and proceeded out over the Mediterranean Sea on the strafing mission to the Foggia area. The squadron and group leaders had to do some very precise navigation to assure getting everyone properly positioned over the target area for just one pass. Having to fly so low didn't help because it limited the number of checkpoints one could spot on land. The reason for the prior strict secrecy was obvious because with our position at such a low altitude, had the enemy known, they could have been airborne at altitude and awaiting a duck shoot.

We stayed low over the water from North Africa to Italy, then flew around the southern tip of Italy and finally saw the spur. After a long wide sweeping turn we were lined up (line abreast) heading in with all our guns charged and ready. None of us knew for sure what our target might be. Hopefully it would be aircraft on the ground, but could be hangers, fuel storage, administration buildings, barracks, or ground equipment.

Despite having passed over two Italian destroyers a few minutes away from the target area we had the benefit of complete surprise. As we entered the Foggia Air Base complex I spotted the tail and fuselage of an aircraft on the ground dead ahead. I gave it a long raking burst of gunfire before realizing my route had taken me directly over an airfield "bone yard" (where all the junked aircraft are kept). About the same time out of the corner of my eye I saw another P-38 converging with my line of flight. He was apparently fixed on a target and would have collided with me had I not dropped down another ten feet. I watched his props narrowly miss my canopy, not being able to go any lower. He must have missed part of the briefing! Lt. Williams in the 71st squadron was hit by ground fire and his plane burst into flames. He pulled up, bailed out, and lit in the middle of a runway on one of the airfields where he was immediately taken prisoner.

My personal effort hadn't been very productive, but we stayed low over Italy on the way back firing at targets of opportunity, such as trains, trucks, and rail facilities. On the way out and over the water my flight met head on with two Me 109s. It occurred so suddenly that both sides pulled up like surprised game cocks. I got a pretty good burst at the lead aircraft, but we didn't have the fuel or ammo left to turn back and pursue them into Italy. (A Greek author, Dimitrios Vassilopoulous, is writing a book at this time entitled *Fighter Pilots of Hellenic Descent*. I sent him a record of this mission, and recently he wrote to tell me German records for that time identified the Me 109 mentioned above as piloted by the Luftwaffe's leading ace, Major Steinhoff, and that his plane was damaged during the encounter. He became head of the German Air Force when it was reconstituted after the war). I have not attempted to make a claim as a result of that skirmish.

Overall we had done some damage to the airfields plus a claimed 150 aircraft destroyed on the ground. The captured P-38 was not located. The First Fighter Group and the other P-38 Fighter Groups were awarded the Presidential Unit Citation because of the mission success.

Chapter 12—Missions Sixteen to Eighteen: Preparing for Invasion

My sixteenth, seventeenth, and eighteenth missions, on August 26, 27, and 28, were similar. We were flying missions every day escorting B-26s to the Naples area to bomb targets such as rail yards, transportation complexes, and bridges. The Allied invasion of Italy was imminent, but the enemy was not sure where along the coast it would occur. On each of these missions we would be met by 25 to 50 enemy fighters and there would be a continuous air battle as we escorted the bombers into and out of the target area.

It is difficult to recall specific happenings to each of these missions, but certain events still are vivid in my memory. During an engagement on one of the missions I looked down to see a P-38 on single engine dive on the tail of an Me 109. The P-38 then blew it to bits—not an easy feat. On return to base I learned that it was Dick Lee, and if anyone could do it, it would be him. When I talked to him about it he treated it as a routine matter; no big deal to him, but it would have been to any of the rest of us. On a mission a few days later an Me 109 pulled directly in on my tail, but was shaken off when our flight broke around in a tight turn and another flight turned into him. Later I found myself in a head-on attack with a Me 109, a condition I'd been hoping to get and much to my advantage. I took a good sighting on him, pressed the gun-firing button and found my guns jammed. The advantage was then his, but he took a short burst at me, then thought better of a head-on confrontation, and did a Split S for the deck. I managed to recharge a couple of the 50-caliber guns before we left the target area but had lost a great opportunity.

On every mission now there was very heavy flak over the target. The German fighters avoided fighting in the midst of their own flak, so when the barrage would suddenly cease we'd know the fighters were on the way, typically diving directly out of the sun. There were sprinklings of Italian fighters generally accompanying the Germans. The Italians were not always aggressive, and in the midst of an air battle it was not uncommon to see one doing slow rolls or some kind of acrobatics off to the side and out of range. By that time they didn't have much hope of being on the winning side and much of their enthusiasm for a fight, if they ever had any, was gone. At a safe distance, they did like to demonstrate their ability to fly, however.

The Germans had learned a lot about us and occasionally used our radio frequencies to call the flight leaders and give them false orders or headings in an attempt to mislead us. They even knew the names of many of the squadron members, including those of some squadron commanders. Our squadron commander, Major Otto Wellensiek, was called several times, but recognized it as a ruse each time. My name was never called because I'm sure they couldn't pronounce it!

In the process of escorting B-26s we lost very few of them to enemy fighters. Most losses were to flak, although on one of the missions to Naples one squadron of B-26s apparently dropped their bombs into some flights below them. It was shocking to see fifteen or twenty parachutes in the air at once as several B-26s went down. Some of our biggest air battles occurred on these missions, and those of us who were raw replacements just over a month prior were now getting to be fairly well seasoned in battle. The Germans were fighting desperately on the ground and in the air to prevent an invasion of Italy (termed the "soft underbelly of Europe" by Churchill), as they wanted to avoid another front on the mainland of Europe at all cost. The "underbelly" turned out to be not so soft.

At Mateur Air Base it was getting awfully hot, and aside from an occasional outdoor movie there wasn't much recreation. We played volleyball for exercise. One day one of the pilots said he had learned of a place not too far away where we could get a steak dinner. That sounded great because we were getting pretty weary of Spam®, dehydrated potatoes, and diced carrots. The Spam® was salty and tasteless despite varied attempts by the cooks to make it more appetizing. The cooks would mix it with other ingredients, dip it in powdered egg batter, fry it, roast it, boil it, and whatever, but it always came out as salty-tasting Spam®. There was a common joke that given our first choice of "enemy" targets, it would be the Spam® factory back home.

With the prospect of a steak dinner in view, several of us managed to wrangle a weapons carrier truck and set off one evening to find the place. It was necessary to be a bit selective about driving over back roads because many of them had been mined by the Germans when they retreated through that area and had not been completely cleared. That seemed a small deterrent at the time to a possible steak dinner so we sallied forth, found the place way out in nowhere, and sure enough they did have steaks. Whether or not they were beef, camel, or someone's pet was questionable, but we didn't try to find out. We had a great time, and not only were the steaks very tasty to us, there was a lot of wine available. We shared the only large wooden table (long and rectangular) in the place with several Frenchmen who somehow got it across that they were part of the Free French underground. They sang "La Marseillaise," we sang the "Star Spangled Banner," and then we all joined in singing both songs. All was serene and compatible until one of our boys, no doubt adversely affected by the wine, took exception to something one of the Frenchmen said and demonstrated his displeasure by hitting him on the head with one of the metal plates our meals had been served on. The French took a dim view of that kind of "friendliness," and the mood turned suddenly ugly. Some of the more sober heads got us rounded up and back in the truck in time to avert a free-for-all, and we jolted home feeling contentedly well fed for the first time since our arrival. Somehow we didn't worry too much about whatever we might have done to Allied relations with the Tunisian Free French. Lt. Nolan, who had wielded the plate, later told me he had taken offense when the Frenchman started talking to him in German.

We found another source for snacks, which helped break the monotony of C-Rations. One of the pilots, my tent mate Lt. Thiesen, had a relative who was an infantry M.P. stationed nearby. He endeared himself to several of us by furnishing canned cheese and crackers every once in awhile. He got them while escorting convoys of quartermaster supplies by climbing on the back of one of the trucks and tossing off a case or two to an awaiting buddy.

Chapter 13—Mission Nineteen: Shot Up

My 19th mission, August 30, is indelibly burned into my mind and was the kind that reappeared thereafter in my worst dreams. It was my first mission as an element leader, and I achieved what may be the dubious record of getting shot up the most and still making it back to a friendly base in a P-38.

We all looked forward to moving out of the #4 Tail-End Charlie position, because as an element leader or flight leader we could expect to be more involved in any action. As #4 we were more or less following the flight around and didn't get to fire much unless the flight got broken up in a big battle. Even then our job primarily was to protect the flight or element leader. We had been escorting bombers repeatedly into the Naples area each day for over a week, attacking targets in preparation for the forthcoming invasion of the mainland of Italy. The missions were almost identical in time over target, altitudes, and strengths each day. On that day I led Blue Flight element of the 94th along with the rest of the group to the Naples area. The mission turned out to be one of two of the 1st Fighter Group's and the war's biggest air battles.

Lieutenant Jim Dibble, a very able and aggressive pilot of the 94th Fighter Squadron, led the group and the squadron that day. He was killed on a strafing mission in Italy a few weeks later. Following the end of WWII his nephew James Dibble and his brother made trips to Italy and obtained the details of Lt. Dibble's final flight. They returned with positively identified pieces of the P-38 dug up from the site of Lieutenant Dibble's crash. In a sense they have become one of us. James Dibble has written about the August 30 mission for various publications. The following quote is his very detailed account of the mission pre-briefing and flight to the target area on the August 30 mission:

*At Mateur Air Base forty odd pilots gathered in the briefing
tent at 0700. Most had just consumed a breakfast of powdered*

eggs and raw, hot coffee, toast, preserved butter, and the like. They sat on rough benches, dressed mostly in the brown summer flying suit of the AAF, and all wore a .45 automatic in a shoulder holster. A few wore summer khaki uniforms, and most sat quietly, smoking cigarettes, and there were the inevitable tension relieving jokes. Each possessed a small notebook and ready pencil. Here the aircraft battle letters, bomber call signs, and homing stations would be entered. And in each would go the start engine time, taxi time for each squadron, and takeoff time. The notes were made with cryptic entries designed to confuse the enemy should the notebook fall into enemy hands.

On every belt was a knife or bayonet the dinghy sticker. It was for the purpose of stabbing the rubber dinghy with which the survival kit of each pilot was equipped should it accidently inflate in flight and jam the pilot up against the controls in such a way to make handling the airplane difficult to impossible. Then there were other survival uses for which the knife might be used.

The survival kits were handed out, and each pilot signed the receipt. They were small. They contained candy for energy, money for bribery or trading, fishing materials, a compass, cloth maps, water purification tablets, a collapsible water bag, and a language booklet.

The briefing was routine and did not last long. The target was the Aversa marshaling yards once again; the escort would be for the B-26s of the 319th and 320th Bombardment Groups.

The pilots dispersed to their squadrons for final instructions from their intelligence officers and squadron commanders, and to collect their parachutes and other personal equipment. Soon the trucks, jeeps, and command cars were driving out along the taxiways to the parking hardstands.

There followed the long deathly wait that was the hardest part of any mission, when watches were checked every few minutes to start engine time, when the stomach felt leaden, and the palms of the hands sweated. Mentally, each pilot computed his missions. Was this the 10th, 30th, 42nd, or his final 50th? It would be one more under his belt in any case, one more for the total, one less to go.

The first Fighter Group climbed out gradually. At 7,000 feet the coast of Africa fell away behind them. Up ahead a line of specks on the hazy horizon stood out, seemingly motionless. Their tails seemed inordinately large. They were the B-26 Marauder medium bombers.

By the time Sicily passed to starboard, the Group was parallel with the B-26s. The fighter pilots found it hard to hold level flight, for the horizon, even at 10,000 feet now, seemed to have disappeared. The flight leaders glanced often at the bombers for reference, and back again at the squadron leader for the same. Then the haze seemed to dissipate a little, and there off to the right was Stromboli showing the black smudge of its volcano.

The bombing altitude was 12,000 feet; therefore the fighters would be flying at around 13,000. The slow climb continued. Suddenly, a heavy line showed on the horizon ahead. It became clearer as the minutes passed. It was expected. It was the coast of Italy.

A humming sound now appeared in all headphones. It rose and fell of its own accord, and it increased and diminished as the fighters wove slightly back and forth. It was the enemy radar searching the sky and fixing the formation.

Arriving at the target area we encountered the usual heavy flak, then a pretty stiff battle with 25 or 30 enemy fighters. The bombers completed their run and left the target area without any losses on that mission. We were also on the way out when someone called in a new batch of "bogies high"—an estimated 75 to 100 new fighters. I looked up to see a whole gaggle of them drop belly tanks and plunge into the middle of us. They had been loitering at altitude awaiting the most favorable time to attack, which would be after we had expended a good bit of our fuel and ammo and were attempting to regroup from the first air battle that day. Following their initial dive into us, a real dogfight erupted during which our flights were completely broken up and much of our squadron integrity disappeared. There were P-38s, Me 109s, and Machi 202s mixing it up everywhere with many losses on both sides. Everywhere you looked there was an enemy fighter or P-38 in a spin or dive, smoking or on fire, some crashing into the Bay of Naples. A P-38 from the 71st Squadron and a Me 109 collided head on, exploding in a gigantic ball of smoke and fire. As one of the pilots described it years later it looked like one of those old WWI movies such as *Hell's Angels* or *Lilac Time*. I saw several P-38s on fire and one, piloted by Lt. Rigney, on fire and bellying into the water off shore. We were not only outnumbered, but outgunned and at an altitude disadvantage. It crossed my mind that we could all be eradicated under the circumstances, but we were not going to go down without a fight. We did our best to protect each other, but our numbers were diminishing rapidly. This encounter tested every bit of flying skill we had learned.

Since our fuel was getting low from the two encounters, our very able squadron leader that day (Lt. Dibble) gave the order to work toward the Bay of Naples and reform as best we could. About the same time a P-38 from the 27th Squadron went by me toward the bay with an Me 109 closing in on its tail. I was alone and broke head on into the 109, firing a good burst at him from close range. He broke off the 27th Squadron P-38 in what appeared to be a fast, uncontrollable, spinning dive. My maneuver, however, had taken me directly back toward Naples and into a beehive of enemy fighters. The squadron, by then, was loosely formed up, out of sight, and heading out to sea.

It was obvious that the German pilots were choosing lots to see who got the honor and there was no way I could best their numbers, fuel, or altitude advantage. I took the only real choice available which was to firewall it and dive for the deck out over the Bay of Naples. Almost immediately tracer bullets started flying by.

At first the tracer bullets were actually converging in front of me and I looked back into a spiral-painted propeller spinner of an Me 109 not more than a hundred yards behind me. As I leveled off at what appeared to be a few inches off the water, he started hitting me. It sounded like hail on a tin roof with occasional large bangs as his cannon rounds hit and exploded. To make a more difficult target, I kicked left rudder, putting my aircraft into a skid and causing his tracers to go over the end of my left wing. As he worked back and started hitting the aircraft again, I would try a skid the other way. This maneuver, taught to me what felt like ages ago by my AT-6 instructor in Arizona, reduced his effectiveness, but he still got quite numerous hits each time as he worked back through. I was so low on the deck that he no doubt had problems avoiding the water, plus my prop wash. At times his bullets raised plumes of water ahead of me, indicating he was trying to shoot from an elevated position and was over-leading me.

It seemed certain my aircraft was either going to lose an engine or explode, and I was considering how to handle that when I noticed I was rapidly overtaking another Me 109 directly ahead and about a hundred feet above me. He was apparently trying to catch up with the other P-38s ahead. That meant that if I went under him there would be two of them on my tail. If I pulled up and eliminated the skid in order to effectively fire at him the guy behind me would have a sitting duck to work on. At that point my chances of survival appeared to be slim to none, so I thought, "If I'm going, I'm taking him with me." I pulled up directly behind the Me 109 ahead and fired all four 50-calibers and the cannon. He started to smoke and curiously went into a gentle turn to the right. Almost simultaneously there was a crash as my pursuer gave me a long burst, enveloping me again with a hail of tracers. One of his bullets creased the canopy bar beside my head, which knocked out the whole rear of the canopy. Plexiglas flew all over the cockpit, some into my mouth. I dove for the deck again, and for some reason experienced no more fire from the 109 behind me. Within seconds, during which I expected to catch more fire, my right engine oil temperature began to rise rapidly and the pressure began dropping. I shut down the right engine and feathered the propeller, then watched the left with no little anxiety. Despite gaping cannon holes in both wings and numerous 30-caliber holes in the engine nacelles and wings, the left engine continued to function fine. Happily the gauges showed no rapid fuel loss. I then made radio contact with the squadron leader, Lieutenant Dibble.

Lieutenant Dibble brought what was left of the squadron around in a 360-degree turn to allow me to catch up. Three of the 94th pilots— Lieutenants Dibble, Pettus and Anderson—stayed with me while the rest of the squadron proceeded back to home base in North Africa. We headed for Sicily, the nearest friendly landfall, and after what seemed an endless time arrived over northern Sicily and proceeded to the nearest airfield.

The airfield was under construction, but there was enough pierced steel planking installed to provide a runway to land on, so I set up an approach. Just as I reached the end of the runway an Italian truck being used for construction drove directly across in front of me. I managed to add enough power to get over him but decided against a go around, not knowing what the condition of the hydraulic system was and whether or not the gear could be raised. (The landing gear had to be raised to effect a successful pull-up and go around on single engine.) The landing went okay, and I had sufficient speed left to coast over to some tents being used by the Army Combat Engineers. As soon as I shut down the good engine caught fire, but was quickly extinguished by an awaiting fireman.

I sat quietly in the cockpit for a moment considering how fortunate I had just been to survive, and to let the adrenalin subside. By all accounts I should have been at the bottom of the Naples Bay. I was exhausted physically and emotionally. During the encounter there had not been much time to think of anything except how to survive it. At one point when it appeared there was no chance of survival, the thought did come over me, *The folks are going to feel bad about this.* As I sat recovering from the adventure, I said a silent thank you to the one who had spared my life.

Climbing out of the cockpit and getting down off the wing took some time. It was difficult to return to normal after that adventure.

The plane looked like a sieve. There were sixty to eighty 30-caliber holes plus four or five exploded cannon round hits the size of a football that in each case flared a large piece of the wing skin up. Even the props had several bullet holes through them. Lieutenants Dibble, Pettus, and Anderson, after seeing me down safely, buzzed the field and continued on to home base at Mateur. I stayed at the field that night and attended a movie that was being shown. The movie contained a Hollywood version of an air battle. I had had enough of that and walked out of it to get some much-needed sleep. The next day I made my way back to the base at Mateur on a C-47 transport. I've always regretted not getting some pictures of the P-38, but doubt if a camera was available. I did bring back some Plexiglas pieces of the canopy found in the cockpit. One piece, very much valued, was carved into a P-38 for me by one of the armorers in the squadron.

I was credited with one aerial victory that day and one damaged. The Me 109 firing at me either ran out of ammunition or broke off to go to the aid of his comrade. The credited kill and damaged were inadvertently listed as Machi 202s, but it didn't make that much difference to me at the time.

We lost Lieutenant Parlett, Lieutenant Peck, Lieutenant Cram, Lieutenant Woodward, and Lieutenant Rigney that day from the 94th Squadron. The other squadrons had similar losses. Lieutenants Parlett and Rigney survived being shot down and were taken prisoner by the Germans. Both of them, classmates, along with Lieutenant Catledge from the 71st squadron escaped, and after months and many close calls, worked their way down through Italy, finally reaching safety and friendly forces in Southern Italy. The 1st Fighter Group was again awarded the Presidential Unit Citation. The air battle was considered one of the biggest of the war, and we later learned that we had tangled with the Luftwaffe's best.

Upon my arrival back at the base I was greeted like a long-lost relative, debriefed by intelligence, and then went to my tent for a much-needed rest—only to find that the air mattress for my army cot was missing! The squadron didn't have enough air mattresses to go around so they were either inherited by the more senior pilots from pilots rotating home, or "requisitioned" directly when someone failed to return from a mission. I was building up a head of steam when one of the more recently assigned pilots came in looking very embarrassed and dragging my air mattress. He sheepishly apologized and it was good for a tension-relieving laugh.

Chapter 14—Missions Twenty to Thirty: The Invasion of Italy

Having been shot up and having lost some good friends left me angry and feeling vengeful. When the briefing for my 20th mission on September 4, 1943, indicated we were to strafe an airfield above Naples, it was evident it had to be one of those involved in the August 30 battle. This time my run took me right down the revetment line on a German airfield. The Germans kept their aircraft pretty well dispersed, but we had surprised them completely. Two very combat-ready-looking Me 109s made a perfect ground target for all four 50-calibers and the cannon, as I watched them both explode in balls of flame. We had no losses, and back home it felt better to know the score had been evened up for the badly damaged P-38 I left behind in Sicily.

For the next two missions, numbers 21 and 22 on September 5 and 6, we returned to pretty much a carbon copy of several of the previous bomber escorts to the Naples area. Each time we were met by 25 to 35 enemy fighters. They always had the advantage of altitude and usually yo-yoed at the bombers or us. They were beginning to be less aggressive however, no doubt saving their resources for the impending invasion. At times they would take a quick downward pass and continue on to the deck without returning.

On September 7 we were alerted to prepare for a move. It was to be temporary, so we didn't fold up our tents. We took enough personal items to be away a week or two. The ground support people had the tough job of gathering up enough of everything to logistically support operations from another airfield.

The move was to Catania, Sicily, and on arrival we immediately began some practice night flying. It was a bit hairy because we were located at the foot of Mt. Etna, which glowed at the top in the dark of night and had been spewing smoke and ashes for several days. Besides bad visibility we weren't familiar with the surrounding terrain. Two accidents happened as a result, both somewhat bizarre. In one case one of the pilots in another squadron attempted to join up on what he thought were the lights of his flight leader. The lights were ground lights, and he hit the surface at around 250 to 300 miles per hour, leaving pieces of P-38 scattered over a wide area. Miraculously, he survived with just the cockpit remaining but no serious damage to himself.

The other incident was a loss of one of our 94th pilots, Lieutenant Phillips, and it was never resolved as to what happened. He simply disappeared on a night training flight. At first it was thought most likely he had crashed into Mt. Etna, but after finding no evidence of that, it was believed he may have experienced vertigo and crashed somewhere in the water offshore.

The town of Catania had been all but demolished during the recent battle for Sicily, and we got a much closer perspective of the effect of the war on the civilian population. They were destitute, many without shelter, and by that time very disillusioned with their leader Mussolini and his German allies. The children were the ones who got our greatest sympathy. The war was not of their making, and they were hungry, dirty, ragged, and many of them homeless. They were begging for food and clothing and often gathered near the mess tent in hopes of getting a chance to go through the garbage cans. Most of them had their heads shaved, the result of a delousing program by our Allied military government. Generally the Sicilians seemed relieved that we were occupying Sicily, as they were better treated by the Allies and the future began to look a bit brighter for them.

My 23rd mission began before daylight on September 9, and explained the reason for the night flight training. We were briefed that we would be covering the invasion of Italy and were not at all surprised to learn it was to be in the Naples area. We were to fly at a certain altitude over the beach and be prepared to take on any enemy air activity that appeared and/or to strafe any targets designated by the ground controller on a ship in the invasion area.

It was a whole new ball game to us. We had had very little practice forming up in the dark and of course there would be a lot of aircraft in the air. Sicily put us much closer to the target so navigation was not a problem. Trucks were parked along the runway with lights on to give us a reference, as there were no runway lights on the airfield. We started up and taxied very carefully to the end of the runway, more or less feeling our way. Just prior to my line up for takeoff, an explosion and fire occurred at the opposite end of the runway. It was obviously a crashed P-38. We took off directly over it, and learned on our return from the mission one of the flight leaders had hit a truck with his wingtip. The truck had crossed the runway at the end of the field. Prop wash from a P-38 ahead had caused the wing to dip and hit the truck just behind the cab. The P-38 bellied in and burned, but the pilot got away from it before it caught fire. Neither he nor the truck driver was injured.

We formed up and climbed out north toward Naples, and within a few minutes began to see the first light of sunrise to the east. As we approached Naples it was light enough to make out a vast armada of ships heading toward the invasion point. I kept thinking about the troops aboard the landing craft and the anxieties they must be feeling. The landing was underway when we arrived over the beach. It was still fairly dark on the beach, but you could see numerous fires inland and among the invading ships in the fleet. We remained over the area for about an hour without encountering any fighter opposition, and then were replaced by other Allied fighters. Smoke and haze on the beach gave indication of heavy fighting and losses by both sides during the invasion. We heard later that bulldozers sent for construction purposes had been diverted to dig trenches for temporary burial of Allied soldiers killed in action.

I flew six missions over the week of September 10-17, each strafing and bombing in support of the invasion. One of these, my 27th mission on September 14, was my first mission as a flight leader, and it felt good to be in a position where I could exercise more of my own judgment and decisions. Our targets were generally enemy truck convoys, heavy troop concentrations, or roads and bridges. The targets were assigned by a controller on one of the Navy ships offshore. On one mission, ground control ordered us to jettison our bombs because enemy fighters were in the vicinity. They never appeared however.

I was assigned to a mission on September 16 but had mechanical problems with my aircraft. After obtaining another and while attempting to catch up with the squadron, a single-engine aircraft appeared quite a way off my left wing. Not knowing its identity I started climbing in order to get some altitude advantage. He did the same and we had both reached about 15,000 feet before his identity became clear as a British Spitfire. A few wing waggles caused him to level off, and since I couldn't catch the squadron it was necessary to return to base. I can't imagine whose side he thought a P-38 with its twin booms and twin engines would be on. He may have heard of the P-38 in German hands and was just being a bit cautious.

By coincidence the active volcano on Stromboli Island started erupting just before the invasion began. We always got a good view of the volcanic activity as we flew over it en route to the Naples area. After completing my 29th mission out of Sicily on September 17, the squadron was directed to prepare to return to the base in Africa. The day before, the German Tenth Army commander had reported back to his base that Allied air and naval superiority had proven decisive. The Germans began preparing to withdraw from Salerno. It appeared to be a turning point in the war, and Allied forces were elated to have a foothold in Italy.

We continued flying missions over the Naples area. Mission 30, on September 30, was to dive bomb a road. It must have been getting monotonous, because my mission log tersely says, "Hit it. No enemy aircraft. Moderate flak."

We had a few days' stand down while getting the group back together; we needed it for some rest. The schedule had been pretty heavy, our aircraft needed maintenance, the ground crews had been worked very hard, and we were ordered back to the more permanent facilities at Mateur Air Base.

Back at Mateur, the 94th pilots along with the pilots of the other two squadrons were advised to don full uniforms on a specified date as the commander of the 15th Air Force would be visiting the base that day and would present decorations to those who had been awarded them. The then Major General Nathan Twining (later to become Chief of Staff of the Air Force) visited us on the designated day and pinned on various awards, including Distinguished Flying Cross medals and a few Silver Star medals. It was also a big photo opportunity day for the group photographer.

Major General Twining presenting
the Distinguished Flying Cross to author, 1943.

*Author with medals;
behind him is a P-38 with
the "Hat in the Ring"
squadron insignia.*

*The 94th squadron pilots pose on the day of
Major General Nathan Twining's visit.*

Chapter 15—Missions Thirty-One to Thirty-Four: Libya and Flight Suits

One day in October while we were playing volleyball, the squadron commanding officer came over, stopped the game, and whispered something in Dick Lee's ear. Dick broke into a wide grin and watched as the C.O. then came over to me and whispered, "You are now a first lieutenant." Needless to say we were pretty happy not to be the lowest on the totem pole any longer. Someone produced some silver bars, which we donned immediately.

Shortly after that the squadron was alerted to move a contingent to Libya. We again moved with a limited support team and had no idea of why the move until we got to our destination. The flight to Libya was interesting because we flew directly over the route on which German General Rommel had retreated. The signs of the tank battle with British forces were very evident; you could see where the tank tracks had churned up the desert. There was a destroyed tank every so often and the entire route was littered with thousands of "jerry cans" (five-gallon cans used to refuel the tanks en route).

We landed at an RAF air base in the Sahara Desert east of Tobruk called Gambut. The field consisted of a runway scraped out of the dry desert and a few tents for living quarters. It was about as rustic as an airfield could be and still be operable. Everything had to be brought in, including our water. Food was very limited (K-Rations), and we were allowed only a half-helmet-full of water a day to clean up with. The wind blew sand in all directions, and before long we were a very scruffy looking bunch. We learned that the Germans had taken the island of Cos in the Dodecanese Greek Islands. This was of considerable concern to the British who occupied adjoining islands, far from their supply support and therefore in serious jeopardy. The British had made the decision to evacuate the islands by ship, and they needed air cover to protect the ships from German aircraft stationed in Greece. The U.S. had been asked and agreed to provide air cover, assigning the 1st and 14th Fighter Groups to the task.

It took a few days to get organized, but on October 8, I was scheduled for my 31st mission as Blue flight leader on a squadron fighter sweep 150 miles northeast of Crete. As we flew over Leros Island we spotted several British troop transport ships on the water. The decks were covered with troops. On further investigation we found some German Ju 88s (twin engine bombers) flying near the ships. My flight flew cover for the squadron leader as his flight attacked a Ju 88. Then, when he pulled his flight up, we took after another one. The ships were putting up everything they had, mostly small arms fire. The Ju 88 flew directly over the convoy at low altitude, hoping we would be picked off by friendly fire. My flight got in several good bursts during which the Ju 88 tail gunner fired back with his single machine gun as they hightailed it for Greece.

Our range was too far to be very effective at first, and as we were just getting in range the squadron commander ordered us to break off and rejoin with his flight. He was concerned about fuel limitations. At any rate I broke off the attack and have always regretted doing so. We got a damaged out of it, but it could have been a sure destroyed had we stayed with it. In retrospect I should have feigned radio trouble and continued to press the attack. There were only two flights of us on that mission and my record says we destroyed one Ju 88 and damaged two.

On return from that area the next day, our pilots heard some excited radio transmissions between the 14th Fighter Group P-38 pilots. They had been scheduled into the same area behind us. En route they had jumped several flights of German Stuka dive bombers on their way to destroy the convoy. The 14th was having a field day as the Stuka was a "turkey shoot" for P-38 pilots of the 14th. Some of the 14th pilots became aces on that one mission. The few Stukas that survived reversed course and headed back to Greece. I was not scheduled for that mission but was envious along with the rest of our group because, although we had some action, we had missed out on the bigger piece of the cake. Back at Gambut we stayed on several more days, keeping the British troop ships covered until they were out of range of the German Luftwaffe.

Following some fierce sandstorms which blew our sleeping tent down and turned everything into grit, we were ordered back to home base again.

A dust storm in Gambut, Libyan Desert, September, 1943.
The tent blew down soon after this photo was taken.

A dust storm in Gambut, Libyan Desert.
A P-38 is faintly visible through the dust.

Our takeoff to return occurred in the midst of swirling dust and sand, and on taxi out I suddenly spotted a barrel of oil lying flat on the ground. I saw it too late to stop or avoid it completely, and the right prop sliced through the barrel three or four times, leaving it spurting oil. A run-up of the engine produced no noticeable vibration, so faced with having to spend several days in the sandstorm, the decision to continue on was easy. The airplane flew with no problem.

On arrival back at Mateur we were trucked into Bizerte, where someone had set up a large trailer van equipped with showers and hot water. It had to be one of man's greatest inventions and was just what we needed. After about two weeks accumulation of sand, dust, sweat, and grime, we qualified as just plain filthy. That shower with lots of hot water and soap has topped any bath since then, even in some of the more luxurious hotels.

My next mission was my 32nd. We flew out of Mateur on October 23 to escort bombers to 100 miles north of Rome. My mission record states: "jumped by 12 enemy fighters. Lost Lt. Lion." My position was White flight leader, but I did not elaborate on the mission. Presumably Lt. Lion, who was in another flight, was lost due to enemy fighter action.

About this time we were transferred from 12th Air Force to 15th Air Force with no change of location but a change in our mission. Now most of our escort of bombers would be high altitude B-24s or B-17s. This meant we would be going longer distances to more strategic targets and at considerably higher altitudes, generally around 24,000 to 27,000 feet. It meant being on oxygen for much longer, experiencing extremely cold temperatures, and operating in rarified atmosphere where we experienced many more supercharger problems with the engines. It also meant carrying heavier fuel loads with larger drop tanks. We were issued electrically-heated suits worn under our flight suits to combat the cold temperatures, often minus 25 to minus 50 degrees Fahrenheit outside the cockpit. The aircraft heater could not begin to comfortably warm the cockpit, and well below freezing temperatures prevailed most of the time above 18,000 feet. The electric suits, plugged into a circuit in the cockpit, were not too effective. No doubt they were the forerunner of the electric blanket as it is known today, but the invention hadn't been perfected that well then. Often there would be spots where the suit burned the skin, while other places were totally unheated. At times, shorts would provide a very mild electric shock. We found that since our legs usually got the coldest we could help some by wrapping copies of the Stars and Stripes newspaper around them.

We also had to become very oxygen conscious. Our system was what was called a demand system; that is, it was supposed to feed in the required amount of oxygen at any given altitude until at some point 100 percent oxygen was supplied. A blinker on the supply diaphragm winked with every breath you took to indicate you were getting oxygen, but it didn't say whether you were getting enough. After losing a couple of pilots in the group to suspected oxygen deficiency, we became very conscious of being properly hooked up to the system and as to whether or not enough oxygen was being supplied. Different symptoms were felt by individual pilots. My best check was to remove a glove and check my fingernails for color. If they were starting to turn blue, I had an immediate oxygen problem requiring a switch to 100 percent until the cause was determined. Usually the cause was a loose mask or a partially disconnected hose resulting from swiveling one's head around in the cockpit checking for enemy fighters. The oxygen supply was not unlimited, so we had to make sure we managed its intake in a way that would assure getting to the target and back down to 10,000 feet or less where it was no longer needed.

For me, it was always a relief to get to a lower altitude because that would provide a chance to light up a smoke after not having had one for several hours. Most of the pilots did smoke cigarettes at that time. The hazards of smoking had not become well known then and it was a means of relaxing after stress. Fortunately I stopped smoking completely about ten years later. That didn't alter my nickname, however.

Mission 33 on October 30, 1943, was to a target near Turin, Italy, as a B-24 escort and as White flight leader. The target was a ball-bearing plant at Villar Perosa. In order to provide continual escort of the bombers, we flew from our base at Mateur to where the bombers were based at

Decimomannu, Sardinia. There we topped off our fuel tanks to ensure enough fuel to get to the target and back to home base. My mission record says, "Flew at 25,000 altitude. Temperature outside the cockpit was fifty degrees below zero. No enemy aircraft sighted light flak." At that altitude we and the bombers created heavy condensation trails which left no doubt to the enemy on the ground as to what our position was, so if there was light flak it probably was because there weren't that many enemy anti-aircraft batteries in the Turin area. We got our first good look at the snow-covered Alps. The mountains were beautiful but daunting, as a forced landing among them appeared impossible. A bailout held no assurances of surviving the snow and cold. Nevertheless, it was a new and different part of the world to see, and a stark difference from the sand and desert country we had experienced in Libya. Unfortunately the concentration needed to fly in formation or to position your flight in a formation did not permit much time to view and appreciate the scenery. After the war and some years later I did get to travel by car through part of the Alpine country and found it every bit as beautiful from the ground as from the air.

Early in November the group commander decided that the enlisted men and officers both needed a club of their own where they could have a place to socialize a bit other than their tents. A project officer was named, and erection of the clubs began, using the only available material and labor, which was packing crates, a few Arabs, and any pilots not flying. Whenever we had time and couldn't escape the project officer, we would lend a hand in building the edifice. The officer's club was finished toward the end of the month and looked pretty good inside with a bar, dance floor, tables with chairs, and a parachute spread out over the ceiling. Various signs were hung about the bar, one of which I show in a picture with Ogden Nash's reflection on ice-breaking, "Candy is dandy but liquor is quicker," a somewhat ironic message since no women were available to frequent the club! We didn't have a source of either candy or liquor except for an allotment of one ounce of rye whiskey each per mission. This ration was usually saved up for a couple of months, and then each squadron was issued a few bottles of Old Overholt rye. It wasn't particularly to our liking, (it soon earned the name of "Old Overalls") but we made the best of it.

Enjoying the pilot-built officer's club at Mateur Air Base, 1943.

We pooled our liquor ration for the grand opening of our club, plus someone had procured a small supply from somewhere to supplement what was available. One of our better-looking and most persuasive pilots went in to Bizerte and successfully invited the nurses at the hospital to attend, so on the night of the opening several ambulances pulled up full of nurses of all shapes and sizes. They all looked ravishingly beautiful to us, and we had a great time dancing up a storm to a local orchestra and downing such luxurious drinks as straight bourbon, straight rye, or bourbon and water, and rye and water. The party ended late at night after we reluctantly put the nurses back in their ambulances and they headed back to Bizerte. We looked forward with great anticipation to another such event very soon but a glitch developed in the whole scheme: our group was ordered to move north about 75 miles to an airfield near Tunis, and the club along with whatever could not be packed up was left to the Arabs.

It was now getting into winter and our tents at the airfield near Tunis were not equipped with any kind of heat. All sorts of heating devices were invented and installed, but the one most used was to burn cans of ethylene glycol. Its intended purpose was as antifreeze for the aircraft, but it was also a good tent warmer and was not volatile enough to explode. Fortunately there was a limited amount of it to use in that manner. The flight surgeons were openly worried about the health of the whole outfit. The ethylene glycol burned a nice blue flame on top of the liquid. It may not have been the healthiest form of heating but it provided at least a minimum of what we needed.

We were sharing the airfield with British Royal Air Force (RAF) Wellington bombers. Our presence caused a severely overcrowded condition in which P-38s had to be taxied about a half mile over muddy taxi strips. Several ground accidents occurred as a result. Fortunately, we were only there a few weeks.

My 34th mission on November 2 was to fly 100 miles north of Rome as B-17 escort, with again no sighting of fighters and light flak. The decrease in fighter opposition became somewhat of a mystery. It was probably caused by a decline in Luftwaffe fighter forces plus some reshuffling and repositioning of their fighters to counter the threat of the imminent Allied invasion of the continent. This required the enemy to prioritize what and where their fighters would defend. If a mission did not encounter fighter opposition at one target area, it could mean that a more important target area would be heavily defended. An example of this would be any fuel supply areas such as the Ploesti oil complex, which was heavily defended with all the flak and fighters the enemy could muster.

This was my first time at leading the squadron, as my record shows my position as Red flight leader. In addition, I was overall mission commander, leading all three of the squadrons in the group. The position, although carrying considerably more responsibility, was easier to fly since you didn't have to maintain a position relative to another flight. Rather the two other flights in my squadron and the Group's other two squadrons were required to maintain position on me.

Navigation to a target was strictly by use of an aerial map and dead reckoning. The aerial maps showed ground features only, so a lot was left to the group or squadron leader in the way of finding the designated target. If we were escorting bombers to a target, navigation was no problem. They did the navigating, we just followed above them. We all carried a small card showing countries surrounding the Mediterranean and a line heading back to our home base location as a backup. If there were strong winds aloft or we were not sure of our position, the cards were not of much use.

On returning from a mission, when we got within VHF radio contact, we had the luxury of a homing communications group that, through the use of radio transmission, could pinpoint the location of an aircraft calling in and give it a "steer" to its home base. The procedure was to call "Big Fence," which was the call sign of the homing group. They in turn would request the pilot to transmit for five or ten seconds, which allowed them to receive from two other stations set a certain distance apart. Through triangulation, they could get a pretty exact fix on the location of the aircraft and give the pilot a heading to his destination.

Return groups of aircraft would sometimes totally inundate the homing station with calls, but somehow they would manage to take care of us. They were lifesavers, and we relied heavily on them to take care of us; it was often with great relief that we received a "steer" from them to home base. They performed untold "saves" and were an essential element of our missions. I have had the good fortune of making contact with one of their members, Ken Dunn, in recent years. It has provided an opportunity to thank him and his unit for the great service they provided. They, without doubt, saved a great many bomber and fighter aircraft as well as the crews.

Chapter 16—Missions Thirty-Five and Thirty-Six: A Homecoming of Sorts over Athens

As November advanced we continued to fly further afield. My 35th mission, on November 6, was as White flight leader on a dive-bombing mission to Marciano, Italy, in which our squadron flew top cover. My record shows "no fighters but heavy flak." The target was the Monte Molino Bridge, which the bombers had repeatedly tried to hit in order to cut off German supply lines, and although we didn't destroy it completely we did considerable damage to it.

On November 15 I flew a very long mission involving staging through Sicily for refueling, the target being Eleusis Airport at Athens, Greece. My position was White flight leader, and we escorted B-24s, which were a much more difficult bomber to escort than the B-17. They were slow, cumbersome, and apparently very difficult to maintain in good formation position as there were always stragglers inviting enemy fighter attack. The more spread out they got the more difficult it became for us to keep them covered. It had to be a very difficult airplane to fly because even the training losses in B-24s were staggering.

We flew to Sicily where we landed and refueled. While we were waiting to be refueled several Italian kids approached and sold us oranges, the first we'd had since arriving in Africa. After refueling we took off again, rendezvoused with the bombers over southern Italy and proceeded on to Athens.

I had aunts, uncles, and cousins in Athens that I'd never met, and I felt some reluctance about being part of a force to do damage there. I had never seen our bombers bomb indiscriminately, so I knew the damage would be limited to a specific target and the civilian population should be relatively safe. As we flew over the coast of Greece and I had the first view of my dad's homeland, I wondered what he would think if he knew where I was at the moment and also wondered what my Athens relatives would be thinking. Meeting my Athens relatives years later when I visited

Greece on several occasions and when they visited here, I was relieved to learn that they had welcomed the sight of Allied aircraft. Their dislike of the German occupation was so intense that they understood removing their enemy would require sacrifices on their part, which they willingly accepted.

As we arrived over Athens we encountered very heavy flak going into the target area, then we were jumped by about eight Me 109s. They were directing their effort at the bombers with the usual yo-yo tactics, but we kept them from getting any decent shots.

We had safely escorted the bombers into and out of the target area and were headed out in pretty good shape when I spotted an Me 109 barreling in directly behind Blue flight. I called "Springcap Squadron, break right now," which was the usual procedure to take counter action. There was no response and the whole squadron just kept boring straight ahead. Realizing there were only seconds before the 109 would be within duck-shoot range of Blue flight led by Dick Lee, I called again and simultaneously took my flight around in a tight turn to intercept the 109. As soon as we got our noses pointed at him, he broke off and started for the deck. I got a pretty good burst at him and then my element leader gave him a long burst. (My element leader later claimed it as a destroyed.) All this took my flight quite a distance out of the squadron formation, and I could hear the squadron leader irritably calling, "White flight get back in formation." Obviously my transmitter wasn't working because he couldn't hear and maybe it was just as well he didn't because he wouldn't have liked my tone of voice or what I was saying.

We crossed over the coast outbound soon after and had no further opposition as we returned to Lecce, Italy, for refueling again. A truck picked us up, and as I jumped aboard, the squadron leader for that mission began to give me a lecture on staying in formation. The lecture got cut short when I explained that he had almost lost one or more members of Blue flight because "someone" had his head up where it didn't belong and wasn't watching for bogies. He got the message and had no comment about my lack of respect for his higher rank as a Captain.

We flew home the same day. My log indicates, "We lost one pilot from the 27th Squadron who I did not know." My log didn't go into detail about losing the 27th Squadron pilot because I had not witnessed the event. It is still a loss, however, and losing any pilot in the group was a loss we all felt and deeply regretted. The flight to Athens had been our longest mission. We had logged a total of nine hours twenty minutes and were given two mission credits.

Danny Darnell, a pilot who was from Texas, joined our squadron in North Africa. He was well liked and often spent quite a bit of his idle time visiting Ralph Thiesen, Ray Schulze, Dick Lee, and myself at our tent. One of his prize possessions was a pair of cowboy boots that had been sent to him from Texas. He brought them to our tent one day to proudly show them off and for no particular reason left them there. They had been there about a week when Ralph Thiesen, who was the more fastidious member of our foursome (to the extent that we sometimes called him "Mother"), decided to do one of his weekly cleanup jobs. These were very thorough and usually took him most of the day, after which his sleeping area was meticulous, tidy, and neat as a pin. It had another affect, too, in that it often shamed the rest of us into at least picking up a few things. During this particular cleanup Ralph found the boots, decided they did not add to the decor of our tent, and took them back to the owner's tent, where in Dan's absence he put them under Dan's bed.

The next day Dan was visiting us when we heard the unusual sound of a pump running somewhere outside. Someone went out to investigate and reported a fire, with fire truck on hand. We all stepped out of the tent to see a fireman pouring water on the smoldering ashes of what a short time before had been Danny's tent and living quarters. We gave Dan our sincere condolences knowing he had lost all his personal possessions, but he drawled, "Wawl I don't really mind because my boots didn't burn, they are in your tent!" We left it up to Ralph to give him the sad and devastating news.

Chapter 17—Missions Thirty-Seven to Forty: High Altitude Combat

The Rome area had some aspects to it that were different from other targets. By this time the Allies had declared it an "Open City," which was intended to spare the Vatican and the city itself from the ravages of war. The Axis forces did not accept the Open City concept, declaring that the city needed its protection. We were unaware of what the "protection" meant, but history has revealed that during the 1943-44 fall and early winter, Hitler had ordered his top commander in Rome to export over one thousand Italian Jews, including women and children, to Germany. When they arrived those who could perform labor were sent to factories to work. The rest were sent to Auschwitz for extermination.

The same madman ordered 350 Italians to be shot in reprisal for an Italian underground action (Via Rasella attack) that had resulted in the death of thirty-five German soldiers in Rome. The unfortunate Romans selected were put in a Rome cave and murdered. The cave was then sealed at both ends. I learned after the war that in the summer of 1941 a brother of my dad (my uncle Emmanuel in Crete) had met a similar fate. He was had been lined up with 100 other men of his age and shot by a German firing squad. The uncle was a doctor determined to make the occupation of Crete as uncomfortable as possible for the occupier.

Mission 37, on November 20, was to Rome as B-17 escort to bomb airfields. We spent a lot of time north of Rome but encountered no enemy aircraft and only light flak that was very inaccurate. My position was White flight leader. The mission took five hours and thirty minutes and was what we would call a "milk run." You seldom recognized a milk run until it was over, so while such a mission was in progress it was necessary to remain alert for whatever might develop. Why there were no enemy aircraft that day was an unanswered question. Quite possibly it was because the Germans were attempting to reposition and consolidate their forces in Italy.

On November 28 I flew my 38th mission and the first to Marseille, France. It was a bomber escort and provided some different scenery from the usual, although most of the flight was over the Mediterranean Sea. Approaching the target the bombers were bounced by six enemy aircraft that were not too aggressive and preferred not to mix it with us. They made the usual quick passes at the bombers then either pulled back up to an altitude a couple of thousand feet above or continued down and away to climb back up later. My notes of the mission describe heavy, radar-controlled flak, very accurate. Some of the bombers were either destroyed or damaged over the target by flak, and there were several of them with feathered engines and obvious damage leaving the target area.

It was often not only nerve-wracking but frustrating to see enemy fighters loitering at a safe distance hoping for an opportunity to attack the bombers uncontested. If we went after them it would leave the bombers unprotected and at risk, the very thing we were trying to prevent. So, while enemy fighters flew at a safe distance and searched for a specific position of our fighter defense that would give them the opportunity to make a quick pass at a bomber without facing our fire, we responded with our own tactical maneuvering. It required our constant weaving over the bombers, with flights crossing in opposite direction to each other. The enemy fighters always had altitude and in-the-sun advantage, which aided them in making a quick pass at high speed and then a return to a safe position at minimum risk. If there was a straggler among the fighters or if we were in a vulnerable position their attack would be directed at one of us. I often wished that we could have the advantage of the defenders in that kind of condition, such as altitude, sun position, and speed. In reality, of course, it was better that we were fighting over their territory, not ours.

At the beginning of December, I was among a contingent of pilots, ground personnel, and aircraft that was transferred to Cagliari, Sardinia, for a temporary period. Some of the ground support personnel remained in Tunisia. We were unaware that we would not see North Africa as a home base again. All of the buildings at Cagliari Air Base had been pretty well bombed out but we found some that, although all the windows were gone, at least provided a roof over our heads. Our sleeping quarters were in a sturdy cement building and we just put our sleeping bags on the floor and made ourselves at home.

The Italians in Sardinia were quite bitter over the war and the bombing of targets near Cagliari even though there had been no invasion or ground war there. When we went into town we were accosted by old ladies lecturing us over the bombings. They apparently thought we had done it. We didn't understand much of what they were saying except when they would demonstrate bombs falling with their hands and, very agitatedly, say "boom boom." Apparently the move to Cagliari was to put us a bit closer to Northern Italy which was now getting a pretty good pasting from all of our air forces in the theatre.

I flew only two missions from Cagliari, my 39th and 40th, on December 2 and 3, both of which were to escort B-17s to the North Rome area. We encountered no fighters and no flak on mission 39 but did run into considerable flak on mission 40. Since no enemy planes showed up we considered both as limited milk runs. My position was White flight and Blue flight leader respectively. The flying time was about four hours thirty minutes for each of the missions.

After only about ten days in Cagliari we were ordered to move again on December 9. No doubt, for us to stay at Cagliari was thought better of, probably for logistic support reasons, so we packed up and moved to Gioia, Italy. The Allied forces had been moving up the Italian peninsula since the invasion in September, and by December controlled all of southern Italy. The war was getting too far away from North Africa for us to be entirely effective from there. We now needed to be further north where we could reach targets in northern Italy and even southern Germany.

Quarters at Gioia were said to have been revamped Italian chicken coops. Whatever they were, they looked good to us because they were wood buildings, accommodated four people to a room, and were equipped with a wood stove and electric lights. The days and nights there were much cooler, and we were beginning to experience winter weather. There wasn't much firewood available so we'd use aviation fuel as a supplement in the stove, a somewhat dangerous practice, as we were to learn first hand later.

Italy, although badly ravaged by the war, was a much better place to be than North Africa. The Italians on the Allied side of the lines by this time had capitulated, and Mussolini had been jailed, then rescued by the Germans and set up as a puppet head in Northern Italy. The Italians were all pretty destitute for food and clothing. Some stores were being opened in the towns and it was possible to go into town and get a shave, haircut, and even a meal of sorts. It was a welcome interlude from the daily powdered egg and Spam® routine we had been on for so long. One evening three or four of us were enjoying a bowl of hot soup in a restaurant. Mine tasted delicious, until the head of a bird—beak, feathers, and all—bobbed to the surface.

Following the successful Allied landings in Southern Italy and Italy's unconditional surrender, German forces had quickly shed their former ally and begun a slow withdrawal to the north. They settled into the Gustav Line, a very formidable and sophisticated defensive belt along high ground at the peninsula's narrowest point. The Germans intended to hold every portion of this line, for as long as they could. A bitter winter followed for American General Mark Clark's 5th Army and British General Alexander Montgomery's 8th Army, mired in mud and with insufficient forces to overcome their opposition until spring.

Chapter 18—Missions Forty-One and Forty-Two: Diary Entries and Rest Camp

Early in December, my aunt Harriet Topping sent me a booklet designed for a person to keep a record of service activity. Primarily it consisted of several blank pages, so I decided to start a diary. With only ten missions left in my fifty-mission tour, I hoped to record the last ten. On December 14, 1943, I sat down and wrote my first entry:

> *Starting this date I am going to try and write the happenings of each day during the last 10 of my 50 missions in order to show some idea of just what happens from day to day.*

Now nearly 70 years later, being older, maybe a bit wiser, and much more conscious of its historical value, I wish that the diary had been kept the whole time during the tour and it had been kept in more detail. One reason for limited detail is that we were continually cautioned not to write anything of a classified nature that might get into the wrong hands and compromise our location or aircraft range and performance. As it was, on my return home I had to surrender the diary to a security unit before leaving Italy. Miraculously it was returned to me after V.J. day. The mission on December 22 where Belgrade is named is an example: I scratched over it, realizing it was classified, but was able to decipher it through the scratchings later. My mission record book was a very small notebook that I carried in an inside pocket so it was not subjected to seizure when I rotated back to the U.S.A.

I didn't fly on December 14. My diary entry reads:

> *Slept in this A.M. for the first time in quite awhile. Slept till 11:00. Schulze (Lt. Ray Schulze) got up at 05:30 to go on a mission over Athens. Ate lunch and spent most of the afternoon fixing up the room. It's pretty sad. Mission returned at 1:30. They hadn't had much trouble except for bad weather. Went into Gioia*

at 3:30 P.M. and took some clothes to tailor. Lee and I got a shampoo and a shave. Shave 3 cents, shampoo 25 cents. They do a good job but I always wonder how they feel about us when they're shaving my neck! We also ate in town and got a shower. Shower felt plenty good first in two weeks. The last had been a bath over in Sardinia. Came home and found several letters.

The next day, we woke up at 7:30, ate breakfast, and went to a mission briefing. At 9:45 we took off on the mission, my 41st, a bomber escort to Bolzano, Italy, just fifty miles from Austria. It was my first trip across the Alps, and I noted that they were covered in snow and that the temperature was thirty degrees below zero Celsius. It was an absolutely wonderful sight from the air. They were so rugged and high it appeared as if we couldn't clear them all at our altitude. That was not a problem, however.

We were escorting B-17s and getting pretty close to Austria and Germany, so we didn't really know what to expect in the way of enemy opposition. Surprisingly the mission produced no fighter opposition, but there was heavy flak over Bolzano. We were short of bombers, I wrote later that day, and only five made it over the target. The mission lasted five hours, thirty minutes, and I made it home in time for supper—which is when we learned the lesson about why not to use aviation fuel in the stove as recorded in my diary:

Lee built a fire at 5:00 p.m. and was pouring gas on it when it blew back in his hand.

Flaming gasoline blew across the room and before we could move the whole room was ablaze. Schulze finally broke out of a window near the stove with Lee after him. McEwen and I were trapped in a far corner for a while, and we could not get a breath. One of the pilots out in the hall saw flames shooting out under the door and threw it open for us just before Lee and Schulze got there. McEwen and I got out by throwing the bed blankets over the flames and running out over the top of them. We all thought it was "finito" for awhile as there was a five-gallon can of gas sitting in the room less than ten feet from the stove. Fortunately it did not catch fire. Dick Lee was embarrassed by the event, but it was surprising that there weren't more such fires. I know he didn't want to add any more life threatening events to our agenda than we already had.

I had several days off between missions, and didn't fly again until Christmas. In the meantime, there was time to explore the town of Gioia a bit. One of the hardest parts of days off was watching the other pilots fly out on missions and waiting for them to return. Sweating out their return was in some ways as nerve-wracking as being a participant. You had no idea what they may have encountered until they returned. When they did, both ground crews and pilots watched anxiously as they counted the number of aircraft returning. Would it be the same number that had departed on the mission earlier in the day, or would there be flights with missing aircraft?

My diary entries for the next several days record life around the base at the time:

12/17/43

. . . layed around most of the a.m. Transport came in with baggage at noon from Tunis, so helped unload it and get it to barracks. Went over to visit Jack Held in afternoon. He lives over across the field. Came back and heated water for a shower. After supper Lee and I popped some popcorn he had got in a package from home. It popped pretty good and was quite a delicacy to us. Some of the fellows had been into Bari and returned about 8:00 p.m. so we spent the rest of the evening hearing about the town. Highlight of the day was steaks for dinner. A real treat over here, and they tasted really good.

12/18/43

Got up at 07:45 for breakfast and had a pilots meeting at 09:00. Talked over our new type of formation and then 8 of us went up to try it. Landed at 11:30. Played poker after lunch until 3:30 then went into Gioia with Lee. Ate supper in there and shopped around at the stores 'til 6:30. Got some Xmas cards. Came home and sweat out another air raid. There was some anti-aircraft fire but didn't see any planes. The anti-aircraft guns flashed like lightning and lit everything up. Wrote letters all evening until bedtime.

12/19/43

Nothing doing today.

12/20/43

Up early and went over to briefing. Mission was to Athens. Sweat the mission off and by then it was lunch time. Wrote letters in afternoon. Kienholtz and Hagenback returned from mission after coming through bad weather which broke up the squadron. Sweat the rest out until we heard they were all accounted for but 3. The others, we hoped, had landed at other bases in the area. One of the 3 missing was on single engine when they hit a storm. Kienholtz said they ran into it all of a sudden and had to break up the formation. He noticed two fires through the fog as he was climbing up. Looks pretty bad as they went into it right near a 1000 ft rise about 25 miles from base. The three missing pilots are Brown, Lipowitz, and Harmon. All new men. Everybody is pretty worried about it.

12/21/43

Up early and flew out on a search mission for 3 of our planes and one of 27th sqdn. Found the one from the 27th where it had crashed on a hill. It was smashed all over the hill and had burned.

Didn't find any others but Hagenback found Lipowitz' plane nearby where it had crashed. Came back for lunch. Ambulance went out and returned at 5:00 p.m with the news that they had located all 4 planes near where we saw the 27th plane. They had all crashed into the hill. Brown and Harmon were both killed instantly. Also a pilot from the 27th. Good news to hear Lipowitz is alive but according to rumor, very badly injured and in hospital at Taranto.

The rest returned from other bases with tales of pretty narrow escapes from weather yesterday. Devenny went through an orchard and had twigs from trees sticking in the tail of his ship.

Hagenback is pretty broken up about it as he was leading the squadron. Not his fault though, and we'd all fly with him anywhere at any time.

Things like the above are hard to take. Outstanding persons, all of them. Two of them married. One of those things you have to put out of your mind for now though or it will get you down. Will never forget fellows like those boys we lost yesterday. Mission tomorrow and I'm on it so will have to hit the sack and get some rest. Weather doesn't look too good but may be ok in a.m. We should be about due to hit Belgrade.

12/22/43

Ate breakfast and went to briefing at 07:45. We were supposed to hit Belgrade today about 450 miles away. Mission was called off just before takeoff because of weather. Our field had about a 50 ft ceiling. Didn't do much during the day. Jack Held came over about 1:00 and visited for awhile. Also had a talk on altitude flying and use of oxygen by a Capt. from Wing Hq.

Some of the fellows went into Taranto to see Lip., but weren't allowed to visit him as he is still unconscious. Has a broken arm and leg plus some unknown injuries.

Lee and I drew lots last night for rest camp. We won so are supposed to go sometime in the near future. We get a week and will spend 1 day in Naples and 5 days on the Isle of Capri.

12/23/43

Got up early and got ready to go to Bari. Went in about 11:00 and ate lunch in town. Walked around the town looking it over. There is nothing in the way of Xmas decorations in the town. Went to a show and saw "The More the Merrier." It was very good. A regular American movie with Italian written underneath. Came home after dark and played pinochle 'til bed time.

12/24/43

Spent most of the a.m. cleaning up and took some cleaning into Gioia. Took a shower in afternoon, which is quite an operation as you have to heat the water with a wood fire.

Tonight is Xmas eve and everybody is pretty homesick. Except for some of the boys who are trying to drown their sorrows. From the looks of some of them I'd rather be homesick.

Some of the pilots were in Taranto today and learned that Lipowitz died yesterday. He never regained consciousness. Scheduled for an early mission tomorrow so am hitting the hay at 10:00 p.m. Guess I'll spend my Xmas on a tour of the Balkans or Germany.

On Christmas Day, 1943, I flew my 42nd mission over North Italy. The weather was bad, which was a constant problem. We just weren't equipped to do weather flying, nor were there ground facilities available for navigation. The overcast made for a confusing, dangerous mission and forced us to spend Christmas night away from our base:

Was awakened early for breakfast and briefing at 07:45. Mission to North Italy. Took off at 9:30 and started on mission. Weather was overcast all the way to target. We picked up wrong group of bombers so went to Bolzano, Italy which is over the Alps. Captain Kipper, who was leading ran out of oxygen and had to return to base, so I took over squadron lead. We were jumped shortly after and had to drop our belly tanks quite a way from target. Flak was very heavy over the target and I saw one B-17 get hit and go straight down. Didn't see any chutes, but heard later several did bail out. We picked up straggling bombers and were just going out over coast when we got jumped by 2 enemy aircraft. The bombers and other squadrons went on while we had to break 5 or 6 times into the two fighters as they attacked. They broke off finally just as we were getting low on gas. Schulze and Griffis got shots but couldn't get lined up. I stalled out before I could get up to the little b......s. Came back through bad weather between overcasts. Lt. Hines reported that he was very low on gas, in fact we all were. Got a homing to closest airport which was 30 miles behind our lines at Termoli, just above the spur of Italy. Was lucky in finding a hole in overcast near the airfield so landed there. Couldn't get gassed in time to go on and weather was bad so they put us up for the night. The 79th Fighter Group (P-40) was stationed on the airfield so they took us in and fed us a Xmas dinner which really hit the spot as we had not had lunch and had landed there at 3:00 p.m. General Cannon flew a new P-51 into the field (The first we had ever seen) and talked to us for awhile about the mission. Great bunch of pilots there. They did everything to make us comfortable. The Tuskegee unit was at that base also flying P-40s, but I didn't get an opportunity to meet any of its pilots.

As previously mentioned, in cases like this where the weather was overcast we relied strictly on homing stations, which would do a triangulation on our voice radio signal and vector us back to base when we got in calling range. They would get awfully busy at times but always did a great job. On this mission had they not brought us over the base at Termoli, just south of the German/American lines, and had we not found a hole in the clouds to let down through, we could have been in serious trouble. The two pesky German fighters that had us breaking into them and doing 360-degree turns all the way down the Adriatic almost succeeded in running us out of fuel.

The flight back to our base in Gioia had its problems too. It continued to rain, forcing us to spend the day in Termoli. The diary continues:

> *Got up at daybreak hoping to get the squadron back to our own base but it was raining and the commanding colonel there grounded us. We preflighted the planes in the a.m. and got them ready to go. Spent the afternoon talking to the pilots in the 79th. They had a small club in each squadron. We heard some new songs on their phonograph ("Pistol Packin Mamma" and "Paper Dolly"). They have a kind of rough life living so close to the lines but get along pretty good considering the circumstances. It was the muddiest place I've ever seen. They live in tents and it was cold as hell. Went to a show in the evening and spent the rest of the evening swapping tales about flying with the 79th pilots. Three R.A.F. pilots wandered in about 9:00 p.m. to visit them. They were from an adjoining field and had been celebrating Xmas considerably. One of them had mud all over his face and clothing and immediately went to sleep in a chair. His buddies explained that "he had become a bit troublesome" so they had to "discipline the bloke." Went to bed at 1130. Still raining.*

The following day, on the 27th, the rain finally cleared a bit, allowing us to take off.

> *Awake early and found the weather considerably better. About a 1500 ft. ceiling. Got the squadron rounded up and by the time we got all the planes preflighted and ready to go it was 10:30. Took off, gave the 79th a buzz job and headed for home.*

Weather was not too sharp. Landed at field at 11:30 and it started to hail. Have spent the afternoon getting cleaned up. It has been sleeting and snowing all afternoon very cold. Got a Xmas card from my sister, Harriet, today.

I didn't write in the diary again until the 30th, when I was briefed to go on a rescue mission to the other side of the Adriatic. Unfortunately, however, I had engine trouble and didn't complete the mission:

Got up and was briefed to go on rescue mission over to the other side of Adriatic. Got in the air, but lost all the oil out of right engine so had to feather up and return to base. Was very "browned off," it was an interesting mission. (secret)

This "secret" mission was to pick up a C-47 crew and its passengers of American nurses who somehow had strayed into Albania. Arrangements were that the underground was to bring them to a remote airfield where two British Wellington bombers were to land and pick them up. We were to escort the two British Wellingtons and try to prevent any enemy action in the area of the airfield while the pickup was in progress. Something happened while our aircraft were en route and the mission was abruptly canceled. We never found out exactly what the problem was but thought the underground had found it to be too risky at the time. We did hear that the C-47 crew and nurses escaped later, however.

On New Year's Eve, I got up early and packed to go to Naples and Capri for rest camp and a much-needed vacation. Dick Lee and I had drawn the full week of time off, and we boarded a B-26 and arrived in Naples around noon.

We saw a lot of Naples in the two days we were there and enjoyed some excellent food and drink at the rest camp hotel on the Isle of Capri. Capri had not been damaged by the war, although with shortages of everything it was undoubtedly nowhere near its normal resort level during our stay. We rode the funicular several times up to our hotel and one day took a trip out to the Blue Grotto, one of Capri's main tourist attractions. We were rowed out in a small boat by an Italian man who kept saying "finito Benito" probably to assure us he had fully surrendered and was on our side. On the way to the grotto and back he held a fish line in his teeth while rowing, hoping to catch an evening meal for himself and his family. When we reached the narrow opening to the Blue Grotto the waves were moving up and down the bank about twelve feet, first covering the opening and then leaving it open for a few seconds. He calmly held the boat at the top of the swell until just the right second, and then rowed like mad to get through the hole. A slight miscue would have spelled disaster, but obviously he was an old hand at it. The Grotto itself was fairly spacious and with just light enough to live up to its name by its bluish color. It was very impressive, although in the back of our minds we had to be wondering if we'd be lucky enough to make it through that little entrance again without being dashed to pieces. No problem to the Italian boatman.

Dick Lee and I had not recognized it, but a week away from the war was just what the doctor would have ordered. We needed the opportunity to get away from combat and experience living under more civilized conditions. The Isle of Capri was untouched by the war and the luxury of a bed with sheets on it and a nearby bath took us well beyond the daily grind at the squadron. A bar with lots of choices for one's favorite libation also added to our all-too-short week of comparative luxury. We tried to forget flying and combat, but in the back of our minds there was a lurking concern about our fellow pilots back at the squadron who were carrying the work load. We didn't know who might be gone when we returned. It was a refreshing interlude, but at the end of the week we were ready to get back to our unit and complete our tour of duty.

Sporting a mustache, the author at rest camp on the Isle of Capri, January 1944.

Dick Lee at rest camp on the Isle of Capri.

Chapter 19—Missions Forty-Three to Forty-Five: Flying Out of Foggia

Dick Lee and I returned to Gioia on January 12, where we found that the 1st Fighter Group had been moved to a base at Foggia, Italy, during our absence. We'd also missed a major encounter.

Map showing area of missions from Foggia

We arrived at our new base to find the group, including our squadron, had been to Wiener Neustadt just outside Vienna and had experienced a major air battle. The entire group participated in the mission, but could only put up a total of eighteen P-38s due to maintenance problems. My squadron, the 94th, had put up eight of them. Badly outnumbered, they encountered some fifty to sixty German fighters in two separate waves near Vienna. Four of our pilots were shot down. One of the pilots, Lieutenant Merideth, made it to Yugoslavia where he crash landed. He managed to make his way back to the squadron in March 1944. Eight pilots out of the group were downed. The 94th Squadron lost Lieutenants

Muffit, Devenny, and Griffis.

Foggia was the area where the Germans and Italians had built numerous airfields. The last time we had seen it, it had belonged to the enemy and we were on the three-group fighter sweep to that area from North Africa in an effort to wipe out as much of the complex as possible.

Author sits in an abandoned German Me 109 at Foggia, Italy, 1944. Photographer Dick Lee.

Author with an abandoned German aircraft at Foggia Air Base

The bases had now been repaired by the Army Engineers and became home to a very large part of the 15th Air Force. Our runway was packed dirt with pierced steel planking for taxiways. It was now the middle of winter, cold and very muddy at Foggia. We lived in four-man tents, heated by a stove manufactured by our own civil engineers from an oil drum. It was fueled by 100-octane aviation gas which we would go down to the line and get in five-gallon cans. The gas can was located outside the tent with a copper fuel line going to the stove. The trick was to regulate the gasoline so that just enough dropped on some bricks at the bottom of the stove to keep a good fire burning. Too much of a gas flow would cause—to say the least—an explosive situation. The condition would have caused a modern day safety expert to turn gray overnight, but it was sanctioned by the hierarchy simply because there just wasn't any other way to provide heat. We used the stove to cook on as well when we could find something to cook. Usually that would be eggs, which we would buy from Italian kids who came by about every day or so to sell them at a price much higher than they could get on the Italian market.

The whole place soon turned into a quagmire and it became necessary to lay boards down wherever there was much foot traffic. Runway drainage was not too effective, and there would often be large puddles of water to negotiate on takeoff. The water, besides intermittent slowing of the aircraft before takeoff speed could be reached, splashed up into bomb shackles and belly tank releases, and then froze at altitude, sometimes making it impossible to drop a bomb or jettison tanks except manually. The good part of being in the complex, however, was that we were near the bombers and could rendezvous easily with them for escort. On a large mission the sky would be filled with bombers taking off and forming up in the area. We could wait until they were just about formed up then take off and join them immediately. There were occasional problems of very heavy traffic congestion when we all arrived back at the same time, particularly if visibility was low.

A refueling truck approaches planes readying for a mission from the Foggia Air Base, Italy, 1944.

Foggia Air Base.

After almost three weeks without a mission, I eased back in with my 43rd mission, a four-hour B-17 escort to Bolzano in which we encountered heavy flak but no fighters. My position was Red flight leader and group leader, leading the group of three squadrons.

The high altitude missions combined with some pretty war-weary aircraft were beginning to take its toll on the number of operational aircraft we could get over the target. Maintenance was scrounging parts wherever they could be found and cannibalizing any disabled aircraft available to keep what we had flying. We would often start out with a full squadron of twelve aircraft and have as many as four be forced to turn back before we could get to the required altitude. The main problem was in the engine superchargers, which were getting an extra workout, but were essential to reach high altitude. When someone had to drop out and return to base we would keep reforming to maintain flights of four and at times found it advantageous to split up into elements so we could keep the maximum number of aircraft crisscrossing in opposite direction over the bombers. I liked the flight composition of aircraft in elements of two because in my opinion it gave us a lot more maneuverability. Generally in any battle we would end up that way anyway because flights of four were too unwieldy.

My 44th mission, on January 21, 1944, was to Marseille, France. I was designated group leader for the mission, which was to escort B-17s. We encountered about twenty Me 109s and FW 190s in the target area. "Ran into quite a few fighters," I wrote in the diary. "Got the most shooting I've ever done. Fired 1200 rounds and ran out of ammunition."

On the way in, as we neared the target area, I spotted an FW190 climbing out to the right of my flight. I turned into him and got a long burst at his nose. He was taking some pretty good hits and pieces of his engine cowling were flying off as he snapped over and dove straight down. We had to stay with the bombers, so I couldn't give chase and in fact couldn't keep an eye on him to see where he ended up. He was claimed as a damaged, but a wingman spotted him on fire so it became victory number two.

Over the target the Germans fighters did an unusual thing. Generally they would move out while the flak was heavy, not wanting to risk any losses due to their own anti-aircraft fire. This time they stayed in the area and continued passes on the bombers all the way in and out. I expended a lot of ammunition before long and during the melee pulled directly in on an Me 109, close enough to be able to see the German pilot as I banked in behind him. His aircraft filled my gunsight circle, and it was certain he was a sure thing. I pressed the gun button and nothing happened. I tried to reactivate the 50-calibers by selecting one at a time and pulling the manual recharging lever but that didn't do any good. My element leader was dutifully holding his fire and by the time I called him to go ahead and fire the German pilot had become aware of his predicament and split-essed to the deck. It was a golden opportunity lost, and most disappointing. Generally our machine guns were pretty reliable, but this was the second time they had failed me, at a very likely cost of a victory in each case.

As we were leaving the target area and things had quieted down, there was a call for help from a B-17. He was just off the coast about 70 miles south of Marseille and was belly landing on the water. We watched the B-17 make a good ditching in somewhat choppy seas. The aircraft stayed afloat for about five minutes, but we did not see any dinghies appear on the water. I was group leader that day so directed White flight to take the squadrons back to base. I then circled the downed B-17 with my flight, called Mayday on emergency channel, and tried to raise some assistance.

There was no answer even when I climbed up several thousand feet higher. Hoping that a ground station had got a fix on me, I noted the position of the B-17 on my map and headed for Ajaccio, Corsica.

Upon landing at Ajaccio and reporting what had happened to operations there, arrangements were made for me to lead six Spitfires with French pilots to the scene where it was hoped we could get a good fix on the location of survivors, if any, and mark it for an air-sea rescue. We flew to the position I had recorded on the map, but found no trace of the missing bomber. I couldn't talk to the French pilots because we did not have the same radio frequencies, plus I doubt if any of them spoke English (and I didn't speak French). We flew back and forth over the area for awhile without finding a trace, and since the Spitfire's range was limited and it was getting to dusk, I finally had to take them back to Ajaccio. We never did learn the fate of the downed B-17 crew. I had some doubts about them having made it to safety. Possibly the Germans picked them up before we got back to them, or they were unable to abandon their aircraft after the crash landing at sea.

My flight stayed at Ajaccio overnight and although dressed only in our flying clothes, we went into the town of Ajaccio and had a meal. The town looked clean and fresh, as the war had not touched Corsica as it had France, Sardinia, Sicily, and Italy. Upon return to home base at Foggia the next day, group operations gave me a mission credit, my 45th, for the rescue effort since it was conducted over enemy controlled waters. The mission lasted about two hours.

The next day, the 22nd of January, 1944, was D Day for Anzio beachhead, which would be a particularly bitter struggle for our ground forces. For security reasons it is a rule in the military that if you don't need to know something of a classified nature you should not be made aware of it until you had a need to know. Such was the case with us regarding the amphibious landing against the Axis forces at Anzio. We probably learned about it in the Stars and Stripes military newspaper. The landing was such a surprise to the Germans that we were not needed until the Allied ground force had consolidated their position on the beach. Intended as an effort to regain Rome, the effort stalled at that point and was unable to advance because of limited forces, bad weather, and a position that the enemy's General Kesselring established in defense confronting Allied forces. Kesselring's commanding position in the mountains where his gunners had a clear view of every target on the beachhead pinned the Allied forces down under miserable conditions until they were finally able to break out of it in May and proceed to the prize: Rome.

A few days later, on January 25, I made the last entry in my journal: "Think I'll close the diary on this date. Can't seem to get around to writing each day. Mission 45 completed."

Chapter 20—Missions Forty-Six to Fifty: End of Tour

One day at Foggia as I was slogging through the mud going from my tent to the flight line, I noticed a group of our troops standing in a circle in a pouring rain. It seemed somewhat strange and then I noticed a figure standing on a bench talking to them and cracking jokes. He was hardly recognizable in a muddy pair of G.I. fatigues, but it was Joe E. Brown, the movie star, entertaining as best he could under the circumstances. I had time enough to watch him for awhile and to form a great admiration for what he was doing. Most celebrities who entertained troops came over in good weather with a great deal of fanfare and a lot of supporting cast, but Joe E. Brown had just modestly appeared alone at the base and was going around entertaining any little group who wanted to listen. I don't think anyone knew he was going to visit us, and he left with as little fanfare. He certainly couldn't have been expected to perform on the miserable type of day he had visited us. I heard later he had quietly done this all over the Mediterranean theatre. It left me with a great respect for him and his efforts to contribute to the war effort.

Mission #46 on January 27 was again to Salon de Provence, Marseille, France, to escort B-17s at high altitude. My mission record says, "Heavy flak. 20 enemy aircraft. Destroyed one Me 109. Picked up flak in wing and 30 cal. slug in nose. Staged at Decimomannu. Had one of our best fights in the target area. Everyone got back o.k." I was the group leader. I don't think I formally claimed the downed enemy aircraft, which I reported as damaged. At some point during the battle I recall diving down on an Me 109 below me but he headed for the deck before I could get to him. It was at high altitude and at high speed, so when I started a pull-out to return to the bombers, I experienced what the P-38 had been noted for, the infamous elevator stall that wouldn't permit me to come out of the dive. Gradual use of the elevator trim, as we were taught to respond, did the trick however, and the nose finally started back up, followed by full elevator control. It seemed like an eternity but probably took less than a minute to bring the aircraft back under control. The mission took seven hours flying time, as we had landed at Decimomannu, Sardinia, to top off our fuel tanks before beginning the bomber escort.

The B-17s and B-24s by this time were hitting targets in Southern Germany and Austria. British General Montgomery, who had been stalemated on a line across Italy below Rome, joined an offensive initiated by American General Mark Clark's forces. Anzio beachhead on the west side of Northern Italy had been established bloodily, but it became clear that the German ground forces were very much on the defensive, although giving up territory very grudgingly. The high altitude bombers could make it to Munich and back, but we could not go that far and still have enough fuel to conduct an air battle. Instead we would pick them up on their way out at the farthest point we could get to and escort them back to friendly territory. These were no doubt tough missions for the bombers, but their missions were coordinated with those of 8th Air Force in England so that the German air defense would be diluted as much as possible.

My 47th mission, on January 31, 1944, was to Klagenfurt, Austria, as escort for B-17s. At briefing it brought audible groans from the pilots because the string on the map went all the way to the top. Our route took us over new scenery, however, as we went over Albania and Yugoslavia. It turned out to be a sightseeing tour as we encountered no flak or enemy fighters. My position was group leader and we logged five hours of flying time.

Things seemed to drag a bit about this time mostly due to bad weather. I did not fly a combat mission for the next week or so. During that time Dick Lee and I were requested to take the piggyback P-38 (a P-38 with radios removed so as to permit a passenger to squeeze into the radio compartment behind the pilot) and go over to Bastia, Corsica, where we would find a repaired P-38 belonging to the group. We were to bring it back to Foggia. On the way over we stopped somewhere in Sardinia at a British air base. The stop was to get some lunch and to switch seats as the one riding in the piggyback position would get pretty cramped after an hour or so.

We found something to eat and returned to base operations to continue our flight when the British operations officer approached us and asked if we would do him a favor. It seemed they had had a P-38 at the base for some time, and although they had repaired it they didn't have anyone who could test hop it. He wondered if one of us would mind giving it a test hop. We said of course we wouldn't mind, and Dick said he would do it. Not having anything to do during that time and feeling that we owed them some kind of favor for working on one of our aircraft, I told the operations officer if they had anyone who would like a ride I'd take him up in our piggyback P-38. The officer thought that was a jolly good idea and immediately produced a young fellow eager to experience a flight in an American aircraft.

Dick and I took off and as soon as Dick knew his aircraft was okay mechanically, he started giving the airfield a pretty good buzz job. I participated also but to a lesser degree because having a piggyback passenger with his head directly over the back of your neck does not encourage the type of flying that might make the passenger air sick. After about a half hour of this, I came in, buzzed the runway, peeled up and around for a landing, and was on final approach with gear and flaps down when Dick, in the other P-38 came barreling down the runway from the other direction at about 300 m.p.h. or more. That was okay with me except we weren't on the same radio frequency and there was no way of knowing whether he intended to go under me or over me. He solved that by dropping even further down on the runway and passing under me. I landed in one direction and got quickly off the runway while he peeled up and around to land in the opposite direction. The British airman loved his ride, but as Dick and I got out of our airplanes the base operations officer met us and said, "That was great, but for God's sake get a clearance out of here quick; the old man is hopping mad and looking for you with fire in his eyes." We had our clearance made out in a seconds, with lots of help from the Ops. Officer, and within a few minutes were on our way to Corsica.

I had heard that another high school friend, Mel Moller, was stationed at the air field in Corsica, so shortly after arrival there I got in touch with him. He asked to be taken for a ride in the piggyback P-38, so I took him up for a flight in the local area. He enjoyed it immensely, and on our return Dick Lee took our picture in front of the plane.

Author (left) and his friend Mel Moller (right), Corsica, 1944. Photographer Dick Lee.

Photo taken by Dick Lee of the author's P-38 while flying from Corsica to Foggia, 1944.

We stayed overnight at Corsica, picked up the other P-38, and came back to Foggia the next day. Within a couple of days we had a summons from the squadron commander, now Major Hagenback. On reporting he asked us what we had done at a British air base on the way to Corsica. "Had lunch and refueled" appeared not to be a sufficient answer. It seemed a message had arrived from the British base commander stating that two P-38 pilots had been to his base and "made a bloody nuisance of themselves." Hagenback couldn't think of a suitable punishment for us, or if he did he didn't apply it. What could he do with a couple of his most senior, experienced fighter pilots with almost all their missions completed? Probably the best thing was to let them finish their missions and go home.

Mission #48, which is not dated in my record book, was to dive bomb a target at the Anzio beachhead, which had just been established. The fighting was particularly bitter there for the ground forces because the Germans held high ground and appeared to have the most favorable defense position at that location. Our squadron was assigned the mission, and we were only able to muster eight aircraft.

I was leading Red flight and Lt. Kienholtz was leading White flight. It was a beautiful, clear day and we were to fly to the "bomb line" (where the Allied forces met the German forces across Italy), then proceed out off the west coast and up to Anzio beachhead. I stayed at about 2,000 feet on the way to the bomb line enjoying the scenery below and noting the destruction caused by the fighting as it had progressed north. We were coming up to the bomb line and about to turn west when all of a sudden the whole sky erupted with very accurate flak. Apparently the bomb line was not where we had been briefed, and we were right over the top of the German ground forces at a pretty low altitude. The shell bursts were so close we could hear them, and the barrage literally blew our flights apart. We wheeled around and up like a flock of shot-at geese. Kienholtz called to say he had been hit, his controls were locked, and he was going into a spin. He was very close to bailing out, but by the time we got around to where we could spot him he had regained control. It may have been the concussion from an exploding shell that caused his problem. I checked out the rest of both flights and found that no one could determine any damage to their respective aircraft so we continued on with the mission, checking each other's aircraft for visual damage en route. The flak was from German 88 mm cannon, a weapon so versatile they could use it very effectively as either an artillery piece or as an anti-aircraft gun. The gun crews that day must have thought they had some sitting ducks because we were flying right down their gun barrels, and they had had plenty of time to get our range, altitude, and any other sighting requirements. We were lucky and I was very thankful that I had not led eight P-38s into what could have been a massacre. We continued on the assigned mission and dive-bombed our target. On return from the mission, crew chief Chet Bala found a jagged piece of shrapnel lodged in the landing flap directly behind the cockpit on my aircraft. It has made a great souvenir. As best I recall no one else was hit. The mission took three hours.

My second-to-last mission, on February 22, was to a target seventy-five miles north of Klagenfurt, Austria. The bombers had gone on to Munich and we were to pick them up on the way out. It took some pretty good timing but after about one circle over the rendezvous point we could see the B-17s as a bunch of dots off in the distance. We were relieved to see them and no doubt they were relieved to see us. We encountered heavy flak but no fighters. The mission took four and a half hours flying time, reflecting the difference in not having to crisscross over the bombers en route to the target. My position was Red flight and squadron leader.

My final mission, on February 25, 1944, was to Austria where we were to again pick up B-17s returning from Regensburg, Germany, and escort them back. All of us sweated out the last mission because to get that far and lose it seemed somewhat tragic. When possible, operations would try to give the 50th-mission pilot a milk run. The missions to Austria to pick up the bombers had not been all that bad, but even so it was an awful long distance over enemy-held territory. The weather was bad all the way to the rendezvous point, making it difficult to pick up the bombers, but we were successful. We found a lot of enemy fighters approaching the bombers when we picked them up, but on spotting us the fighters maintained a discreet distance. Three of them made harassing passes but did no apparent damage.

On the way out, one of the other pilot's aircraft caught fire, and he was forced to abandon it. It was Lieutenant Gresham from the 71st squadron who had been hit, possibly by flak as we joined the B-17s. He bailed out over Yugoslavia. Later it was learned that he had been captured by two Yugoslavian civilians loyal to the Germans. On their way to the German forces he was left alone with one of his captors who went to sleep while guarding him. Lieutenant Gresham was able to knock him unconscious with a rock, steal his pistol, and make good an escape to friendly Yugoslavian partisans. My position for the final mission was squadron leader. Flight time was five hours and fifteen minutes.

As usual Jack Held and Sergeant Bala met me on landing, this time accompanied by the squadron commander and several other pilots. Sergeant Bala saw a much more confident and seasoned pilot than the one he had strapped in almost nine months prior to fly a dive-bomb mission to Sicily. My missions actually numbered fifty-one, since we were given double credit for #36 (Athens mission) because of its length.

Dick Lee finished up almost simultaneously with me. We were required to hang around the squadron for a couple of weeks during which we anxiously awaited orders to return us stateside. During that time we made a lot of trips into the town of Foggia and killed time any way possible. Finally our orders arrived, and as we picked them up at group headquarters the group executive officer said, "Now listen, headquarters at Bari is getting fed up with returning pilots coming up there asking if their promotion orders have arrived. Just go to Bari, arrange for your transport out and don't bother those people. If you have promotion orders they will be forwarded to you back stateside." We both answered with a convincing-sounding, "Yes, sir."

Back at the squadron it was hard to say goodbye to the ground crew and to our fellow pilots. We'd been through a lot with most of them and with all of them we had formed a bond almost like that of a brother. That bond remains as strong today as it was then.

Dick and I discussed the promotion situation on the way to Bari and decided there was something fishy about it, and whether we bothered some headquarters personnel officer or not we were going to at least ask where we stood. So on our arrival in Bari we somewhat timidly appeared at 15th Air Force Headquarters and found the promotions section in Personnel. A lieutenant colonel ground officer met us, and although we expected to lose our heads, he answered our promotion question with, "Let me check that out."

He came back in a few minutes and said, "You are both on the promotion list but your travel orders shipping you out of the theatre negate the promotion. He paused just long enough to observe a couple of crestfallen lieutenants and then said, "Tell you what, if you are willing to wait around until tomorrow I'll have your travel orders rescinded, we'll then cut promotion orders on you and give you a new set of travel orders dated after the promotion orders." We didn't find it a bit difficult to agree to that and promised to be back the next day at 3:00 p.m. as he had suggested. He was as good as his word and the next day he handed us a new set of orders and seemed pleased to watch us pin captain bars on each other. We thought he was about the finest personnel officer in the entire Air Corps.

Our orders directed us home by way of Casablanca where we were to proceed by ship. We caught a C-47 transport to Casablanca, and while awaiting a ship Dick talked himself on to a Navy transport and flew home. I for some reason decided to conform to the travel orders and after about a week or ten days left Casablanca on an old cement-hulled victory ship along with several other pilots rotating home from the other two P-38 fighter groups in the theatre. We joined a convoy out near the Azores and slowly splashed our way across the Atlantic for what seemed forever.

Our arrival in New York about fifteen days later was like entering a new world. It was foggy at sea when we arrived and the first sight of good, secure, un-bombed U.S.A. was the Statue of Liberty with the fog swirling around her feet. We were let out on the city where we enjoyed such things as fresh veggies, steak, hamburgers, showers, and the sight of pretty American girls, not to mention taxi cabs, ice cream, and candy bars. So much had happened since leaving for overseas it seemed like I'd been gone an eternity. Of the group of pilots who had boarded the train in Los Angeles the previous May en route to the first leg to Africa, less than half returned. Some, however, were in prison camps and returned after the war.

The Distinguished Flying Cross, the Air Medal with eight oak leaf clusters, three campaign ribbons, and two Presidential Unit Citations felt pretty good on my uniform along with the newly-acquired captain's bars. No time was lost sending a wire home saying, "Put the pot on the stove, am on the way home."

Chapter 21—Stateside

The pure joy of seeing one's family again and experiencing their delight at having me back is beyond my ability to express. After a week or two at home and another week at a rest hotel in Santa Monica, orders assigned me to Ontario Air Base, California (now Ontario International), as a P-38 flight instructor. We checked out new pilots and gave them combat training prior to their shipment overseas. Each instructor was assigned four student pilots who were taken through all phases of check out and combat training in P-38s. A diversion from the norm was to take them on a formation flight down through Death Valley after which they could then say they had flown at an altitude below sea level. All the instructors, some from my overseas fighter group, had had a tour of combat. We felt duty bound to get the newbie pilots in a much better position to face combat than we had initially been.

Just as I was about to be sent to another combat tour, the end of the war in Europe and Japan closed that possibility and a very eventful chapter in my life. On Victory Japan Day another pilot and I drove in to Hollywood to see what was happening. It was a madhouse of people on the streets celebrating the end of a very difficult time for all. As we walked down the jammed street toward landmark Hollywood and Vine Streets, we were hugged, kissed, and thanked by grateful citizens. The whole country suddenly felt the enormous relief of the end of sacrifice, a hard fought war, and the disastrous threat of Hitler and Tojo.

Ontario Army Air Base was deactivated shortly after V.J. Day and, although it was a time of rejoicing, it also brought on a sadness at seeing one's flying buddies being discharged from service and disappearing in all directions back to their home towns. They had become lifelong friends. The instructor pilots who were married had brought their wives and lived near the base, so we were not only close at our work, but socially as well. It was difficult to see them leaving, with the thought our paths might never cross again. The pressure, and at times anguish, of wartime activity had suddenly ceased. Our lives had been swept up by world events, but now we had to think about peacetime, and what the future might hold for us.

Epilogue—A Life in the Military

I was torn as to whether to remain in the Air Corps or to re-enter civilian life, but decided to stay on for a while and see how things developed. That decision was the start of a 32-year career in the active Army Air Corp, and USAF with one short break. Every chance I could, I tried to get flying assignments. The military often had other ideas.

The sudden discharge of a great majority of ground officers left the Army Air Corps extremely short of support personnel, while at the same time there was a surplus of pilots. The pilots who remained at Ontario A.B. were shipped to various bases, in my case to Portland Army Air Base in Oregon. Given the sudden shortage of ground officers, many pilots found themselves assigned to primary duties other than flying. It was a struggle just to get one's minimum flying time for the month, and that had to be done in whatever type aircraft available.

Soon after arrival in Portland, I was called to base headquarters, where I was informed that my background in accounting made me the obvious candidate for the base Purchasing and Contracting Officer. When I reported to the Base P&C Office, the departing P&C officer, a lieutenant colonel, stacked about a foot of regulations and directives on his desk, and on his way out the door said, "Read these, I will be discharged in three days but have been tagged to inventory the commissary in the interim." I never saw him again. Fortunately the civilian office clerk was very capable, and she kept me out of trouble in many situations that were over my head.

During my six-month stay at Portland A.B., I met the love of my life, Jane Good. She came from an established, Oregon family whose ancestors had migrated to Oregon over the Oregon Trail in the mid-1800s. Honey-blond hair, a sparkling personality, an infectious dimpled smile, and a willingness to put up with me resulted in our marriage just a few weeks after I had received orders to Japan, but she was willing to accept that condition. She, over the years, has presented me with two boys and two girls who have each contributed to a great family makeup. During combined four years of remote tours without the family and/or awaiting housing at overseas bases, she very ably managed the children and family affairs. The four offspring, now adults, have all met our greatest expectations.

My overseas orders were of an urgent nature, sending me by air to Air Corps Headquarters in Japan, there to be further assigned to a P-61 night-fighter unit. When I reported in at Air Corps Headquarters, the personnel officer asked, "Why are you here?" When I told him about the urgent orders, he said, "We don't need you for that. Do you have any other preference?" When I suggested a P-38 unit, he informed me that the Air Corps had eliminated all P-38s from their overseas inventory. P-51s were now the preferred fighter because they were considered more advanced and easier to maintain. Given a choice of the P-51 squadron at Johnson Air Base (near Tokyo) or one near Seoul, Korea, I opted for the 35th Fighter Squadron at Johnson A.B. I had flown P-51s for a short time at a Florida gunnery school, so the transition was not difficult. The P-51 was a great fighter aircraft, but it never replaced my endeared P-38.

Author with a P-51 in Japan, 35th Fighter Squadron, 1947.

The mission of the 35th P-51 squadron was primarily training, but on occasion we would provide escort for Russian transport aircraft through the Russian corridor in and out of Japan. They had a habit of "straying" off the designated corridor, always with a camera at every window. We would nudge them back on track. The assignment also permitted an opportunity to fly over Hiroshima and view the staggering destruction of that city by the A-bomb. A favorite pastime on local flights was to fly in and out of the Mt. Fuji crater.

Jane had not been authorized to accompany me to Japan because of a shortage of base housing, but I was told to expect available housing in six months. When that period was up, I was told it would be another six months, so I called Jane to tell her the disappointing news. We both agreed that, since I was eligible for discharge from the service, I should do so and return home. I was on my way within a week or two, this time by much slower transport, a troop ship.

Jane met me when we docked at San Francisco and we proceeded to Beal A.B. in Northern California for discharge processing. Upon completion of processing I was offered what was called a "gang plank" promotion to major if I stayed in the reserve. It was a good way to keep a hand in at flying, so I accepted it. Advancing from second lieutenant to major in four years wasn't too bad either.

Four years (1947-1951) of civilian life and reserve duty as a "weekend warrior" at McClellan A.B. (Air Materiel Command) in Sacramento passed before the Korean conflict caused my recall to active duty. It became obvious that if I stayed in as a reservist in what had by then become a separate service (the U.S. Air Force), I would be in and out of it for the next twenty years or more. That didn't appear to be the way to further one's career in either the civilian or military category, so I chose to remain in the Air Force and later accepted a regular commission in place of the reserve status.

I had hoped to return to an operational fighter unit, but my years primarily tagged as a logistics officer in Air Material Command resulted in an assignment in 1951 to Kadena Air Force Base in Okinawa as a transportation officer. I continued flying as much as was permitted, but it was a secondary duty. My flying for the next several staff assignments consisted mostly of making administrative flights in WWII-type C-47s, the "Model A" workhorse, as a cargo and passenger aircraft in the Air Corp and then Air Force for many years. It was not a speedy aircraft, so the fighter pilots of that time joked that the C-47 (Gooney Bird) was the only Air Force plane that received bird strikes from the rear!

The logistics tag over the course of my career would mean assignment in that capacity to two division headquarters, two major command headquarters, and a major combined services headquarters. I adapted to staff work well, but disliked it. The cold war was on and everything required of a staff officer had to be done with a short deadline, causing a lot of pressure. I wanted to get back to primary flying duty, but the personnel people at all command levels seemed to prefer I stay in the logistics field.

Air Force Personnel's preference was repeated after the Okinawa tour by assigning me to a logistics staff position at Ent A.F.B. in Colorado Springs in 1953. While in Air Defense Command Hq. there, I did get a chance to check out in a T-33, my only jet-powered aircraft experience. This raised my hope that I might get back to flying, so I applied to fly F-89s when an opening appeared. Personnel okayed the assignment provided that Air Defense Command could replace my staff position there from internal resources. That in effect shot it down because Air Defense Command did not have that resource.

The next assignments were to 12th A.F. Division Headquarters at Ramstein A.F.B., Germany, in 1956 and USAF Hq. at Wiesbaden from 1957 to 1959. Soon after I arrived at Wiesbaden, a directive arrived from Air Force Hq. stating that all pilots who had not reached command pilot status (3,000 flying hours) within fifteen years of pilot-rated service would be grounded in the near future. I fell into that category. That news was devastating. I had made numerous attempts to return to a primary flying job, but personnel had turned me down, saying I was required in the logistics field. Now I was being punished for not having flown enough. It was also grossly unfair to fighter pilots because flying time in fighters, for obvious reason, builds very slowly as compared to transport or bomber pilot's time.

The general in charge of logistics at the headquarters (my boss's boss) understood the dilemma and agreed I should be permitted to get as much flying time as possible prior to the deadline date. I flew the available C-47s as much as I could, often over weekends, while holding down my logistics job. The flights took me all over Europe and to some Mideast countries. Prior to the end of my tour, I accumulated the required flying hours and was awarded command pilot wings. As the general pinned them on me, I thought I was home free.

I finally convinced a personnel officer at Wiesbaden that I should get back to a primary flying job. My age by then militated against flying fighters, but he was successful in getting my next assignment to a Military Air Transport unit at Dover A.F.B., Delaware, to fly C-124 (Globemaster) transports. Finally, flying was my primary duty and I was back in the cockpit.

I couldn't believe what I saw when the Dover A.F.B. squadron commander took me to the flight line to show me a C-124. We climbed a ladder to get into the cargo and passenger bay. The size of the bay was huge, particularly compared to any other transport aircraft or the other small planes I had flown. The cargo area looked like the inside of a warehouse. Another climb up a ladder brought us to the cockpit, which was also enormous, and we were then fifteen feet off the ground. The cockpit area, in addition to pilot and co-pilot positions, provided a space for a flight engineer and navigator. Behind that was a sleeping bunk, used for augmenting crew members. In the cargo bay a loadmaster supervised the loading and unloading of the aircraft and managed the cargo during flight as part of the crew. With four of the largest aircraft gasoline-driven engines produced for the Air Force and a long range, the C-124 had been the workhorse transport of the airlift command for a number of years. The wings were thick enough to permit the engineer to crawl out and stand behind the inboard engines to remove an overheated generator in flight.

Just as I was being assigned to C-124 check-out at Oklahoma City, the list of those pilots eliminated from flight status by USAF Hq. came out. I was on the list. Anger and frustration reigned again, and I came close to requesting retirement from the Air Force. After a week or so word came down cancelling the directive. The reason, it was learned later, was that the commander of Missile Command had gone to USAF Hq. with the news that his command would be devastated by the directive because most of his assigned engineers were pilots who also could not meet the Air Force dictate. They would leave en masse if grounded as pilots. USAF Hq. had seen the light!

Check out at a special C-124 school was arduous, but thorough. The biggest difference was that in that type of aircraft the pilot in command of the flight is constantly in the process of directing a large crew. Until cruise altitude and level off was reached, it required almost continued direction and response by a rolling check list. Except for rare formation flying, the pilot managed the four throttles on takeoff, final approach, and landing only. The rest of the time power and propeller settings were called out to the engineer who then set them accordingly. Despite an applicable emergency procedure, it left me with the impression that if we ever lost our intercommunication capability in flight, we would simply fall out of the sky!

Stationed at Dover from 1959 to 1961, I experienced a lot of interesting flying over the Atlantic to Europe, Greenland, and India. A highlight of that assignment was a temporary assignment of our squadron to Chateauroux, France, in 1961. From there we airlifted United Nation troops to and from the Belgian Congo when that country experienced an uprising against its Belgian occupants.

A C-124, with open cargo bay doors, at a refueling stop en route to Belgian Congo, 1961.

The C-124 dwarfs smaller planes on the tarmac at a refueling stop en route to Belgian Congo, 1961.

In 1962, I was selected to attend the Armed Forces Command and Staff College at Norfolk, Virginia. On completion I was pleased to be assigned to a C-124 Squadron at Travis A.F.B., California, and to have the opportunity to fly the Pacific area which included destinations to Hawaii, Vietnam, the Philippines, Korea, Japan, and numerous Pacific Islands. On one trip to Vietnam my schedule was changed, and I continued on around the world by way of New Delhi, India, my first and only around-the-world trip.

During the three years at Travis A.F.B. (1962 to 1965), I was promoted to lieutenant colonel. I had become one of the Air Force's most senior majors, because a few years after attaining that rank, Air

Force implemented a policy that unless one could walk on water and leap over tall buildings, a total of seventeen years commissioned service was required before being considered for lieutenant colonel. Like most, I was not good at walking on water and could barely leap over an orange crate, so that was out. Being stuck at the major rank beat working up little by little over seventeen years in the mostly peace time Air Force, however.

Shortly thereafter Personnel struck again. I was about to go to transition school to be checked out in the C-141, the command's first all-jet cargo aircraft, when orders arrived transferring me overseas. The orders specified my assignment as commander of an Aerial Port detachment at Kimpo A.B. near Seoul, Korea. My squadron commander was upset by that turn of events, as was I, but despite his best effort to retain me the orders stood.

The assignment was considered a remote tour; therefore, it was limited to a one-year term with no dependents. After settling the family at the nearby city of Vacaville, I departed for my new assignment in August 1965. It was gratifying to have a command assignment, but disappointing too, because I knew my days of flying as a primary duty were over. On the plus side the assignment was interesting since the detachment operated the main Air Force terminal for cargo, troops, and embassy personnel in and out of Korea. I had a very accomplished staff of junior transportation officers, NCOs, and enlisted personnel, so the unit ran smoothly and efficiently.

My attendance at the tri-service Armed Forces Staff College brought on the inevitable, so at completion of the tour in Korea in August 1966, I was assigned to the combined Army, Air Force, and Navy command then called Headquarters Strike Command located at McDill A.F.B. in Tampa, Florida. At this writing the name has been changed to Central Command, and it has the job of directing the wars in Iraq and Afghanistan.

It was an interesting and valuable experience to work with members of the other services. An Army major who worked with me in my office continued on to four-star general rank and became the Director of

Logistics at Army headquarters during our first war in Iraq.

The Vietnam War was in full swing at this time, and I felt that I was somewhat out of the loop as far as the Air Force was concerned. I applied to Air Force Headquarters Personnel for a tour flying C-47 gunships, but was denied that assignment. Instead, in August 1969, I was assigned to the 2nd Aerial Port Group Headquarters located on Tan Son Nhut A.F.B. at Saigon, Vietnam. This was another unaccompanied tour with the family settled at Vacaville, California, during my absence. About six months after my assignment there as plans officer, I was surprised to find my name on the colonel's promotion list. I pinned on the Eagles in early January 1970 and became vice-commander of the Group.

Our job at the Aerial Port Group Headquarters was to oversee the operation of three Aerial Port Squadrons, which in turn operated fifty-two detachments on air bases and airstrips throughout southern Vietnam in support of the airlift force assigned to that theatre of war.

My next assignment took me to Langley A.F.B., Virginia, where I performed from 1970 to 1973 as Vice-Commander and Commander of the 1st Aerial Port Group Headquarters and its three squadrons. About two years after my assignment to Langley A.F.B., Air Force came out with a directive which discontinued flying status of those of a certain age and specialty. The handwriting was clearly on the wall. I was not going to fly in the Air Force anymore, even administratively, and my chances of furthering my career after a total of thirty-two years of active and reserve duty stood pretty much at a standstill. I decided to retire and took retirement from the Air Force on June 30, 1973.

It had been a great career, and as I drove out the gate for the last time my thoughts turned back to the past. So much had changed since I grew up in the little village of Proberta. The Great Depression had left me with no great expectations of a career in any field. The goal at that time was just to get a job, any job that would sustain one, and then hope that it would lead to some kind of future. My life had taken a totally unexpected turn with the advent of military selective service, resulting in a career so remote that I had never dreamed of it. Events took me to the sky in an occupation that I had found fascinating and loved. To quote an unknown: "Once you have tasted flight, you will forever walk the earth with your eyes turned skywards, for there you have been and there you will long to return."

Despite my frustration over not being allowed to remain in flying as a primary duty, my career had progressed well—culminating in senior officer status. Again, as many times before, my thoughts turned back to flying the P-38 and the great group of people I had been privileged to serve with in combat. I thought of the real heroes of WWII and all wars— those who had not returned.

It has been possible to detail here only some of what happened to me as a pilot during WWII and thereafter. As a fighter pilot in P-38s I had been blessed to have flown such a great airplane. The air war tends to appear glamorous compared to other forms of combat, but as Georges Clemenceau once wrote, "War is a series of catastrophes." During combat we witnessed and felt those tragedies, but at the time had to harden ourselves to the loss of some very close comrades. When one was lost we tried not to dwell on it, generally referring to it tersely as "he augured in" or "bought the farm." That didn't mean that he was forgotten; it meant that we had to put the grief of the loss of a comrade on the back burner until the war was over.

In the early 1970s, a 1st Fighter Group Association was formed and a great many of the WWII group have reunited at a reunion held every two years. It is like a reunion of brothers. Doug Campbell, a WWI 94th Fighter Squadron ace, attended the early reunions. He told us about shooting down his first German biplane, after his squadron received a phone call saying a German aircraft was headed their way. He had time to take off and intercept the enemy plane with his Spad. The speed of aircraft and technology over time has changed that procedure considerably. Now the approaching aircraft would have arrived and departed before the phone could be answered. In later reunions the post WWII 94th Fighter

Squadron pilots, flying jets, must have considered us as somewhat prehistoric, much as we had viewed Doug Campbell in his day and age. Our reunions have again brought us together along with our wives and occasionally a member's offspring. I had the pleasure of socializing with most all of the old "gang," getting reacquainted with aces Dick Lee and Jack Ilfrey from the 94th Fighter Squadron and another great person and ace, Tom Maloney, from the 27th Fighter Squadron

There is a special bond between us at the reunions, be it crew chief, company clerk, pilot, supply clerk, or the guy who tried desperately to make Spam palatable. Our numbers have greatly diminished over the years but the bond seems every bit as strong today or maybe even stronger than it was back when we depended so heavily on each other for our very survival. We pause briefly at the reunions to remember, and all feel a deep sadness and sense of loss for those who were lost in action, having made the supreme sacrifice in the very prime of their lives.

About the Author: Robert "Smoky" Vrilakas

Following 32 years in the U.S. armed forces, Robert "Smoky" Vrilakas retired from the Air Force in mid-1973. He later launched a specialized machine shop in Portland, Oregon. Robert turned the shop over to his two sons in 1980 and took up fishing and golf as his primary duties.

Retired as a command pilot with over 9000 hours flying time and 51 combat missions, Robert has flown a number of different military aircraft including:

Stearman PT-17

Vultee BT-13

North American AT-6

Curtis Wright AT-9

Lockheed P-38

North American P-51

Lockheed T-33

Douglas C-47

Douglas C-124

Douglas C-118

In addition, these are his flight qualifications:

Aircraft Commander

Instructor Pilot

Flight Examiner

2 aerial victories

2 damaged in the air

2 destroyed on the ground

Robert Vrilakas held these command positions:
Detachment Commander
Aerial Port Group Vice Commander
Aerial Port Group Commander

He was awarded several decorations:
Joint Service Commendation Medal
Air Force Commendation Medal
Presidential Unit Citation (2)
Legion of Merit
Bronze Star Medal (1 oak leaf cluster)
Air Medal (8 oak leaf clusters)
Distinguished Flying Cross

Robert "Smoky" Vrilakas
May 2010

Acknowledgments

My thanks to my entire family for their encouragement, support, and valued assistance.

And my thanks to my daughter Cindy Simons and grandson Eric Simons (authors themselves), without whose patience and guidance this would not have been possible.

Thanks to Bob Lee and Ken Meyers for sharing their photos and to Jim Dibble for sharing his excellent description of a mission briefing and escort to the target.

CPSIA information can be obtained
at www.ICGtesting.com
Printed in the USA
FSOW02n0938150115
4518FS

9 781935 354475